On the Old Testament

A Book You'll Actually Read

Also available in the series:

On Who Is God?
On Church Leadership
On the New Testament

A Book You'll Actually Read

On the Old Testament

Mark Driscoll

CROSSWAY BOOKS

WHEATON, ILLINOIS

On the Old Testament
Copyright © 2008 by Mark Driscoll

Published by Crossway Books
      a publishing ministry of Good News Publishers
      1300 Crescent Street
      Wheaton, Illinois 60187

Interior design and typesetting by Lakeside Design Plus
Cover design and illustration by Patrick Mahoney
First printing 2008

Printed in the United States of America

Trade Paperback ISBN: 978-1-4335-0135-7
PDF ISBN: 978-1-4335-0444-0
Mobipocket ISBN: 978-1-4335-0445-7

Library of Congress Cataloging-in-Publication Data
Driscoll, Mark, 1970–
    On the Old Testament / Mark Driscoll.
        p. cm.—(A book you'll actually read)
    Includes bibliographical references.
    ISBN 978-1-4335-0135-7 (tpb)
    1. Bible. O.T.—Introductions. I. Title. II. Series.

BS1140.3.D75   2008
221.6'1—dc22

                                      2008000503

VP	16	15	14	13	12	11	10	09	08
	9	8	7	6	5	4	3	2	

Contents

Minor Prophets (Hosea, Joel, Amos, Obadiah, Jonah, Micah, Nahum, Habakkuk, Zephaniah, Haggai, Zechariah, Malachi)

Series Introduction

On the Old Testament is part of an ongoing series of books you will actually read. The average person can read these books (minus the appendixes) in roughly one hour. The hope is that the big truths packed into these little books will make them different from the many other books that you would never pick up or would pick up only to quickly put down forever because they are simply too wordy and don't get to the point.

The A Book You'll Actually Read series is part of the literature ministry of Resurgence, called Re:Lit. Resurgence (www.theresurgence.com) is a growing repository of free theological resources, such as audio and video downloads, and includes information about conferences we host. The elders of Mars Hill Church (www.marshillchurch. org) have generously agreed to fund Resurgence along with the Acts 29 Church Planting Network (www.acts29network.org) so that our culture can be filled with a resurgence of timeless Christian truth that is expressed and embodied in timely cultural ways. Free downloads of audio and/or video sermons by Pastor Mark Driscoll on topical issues and entire books of the Bible are available at www.marshillchurch.org.

Introduction

Like many kids, I grew up with a few bits of Bible trivia, such as the shepherd boy David defeating the giant warrior Goliath, and a vague awareness that people such as Abraham and Moses were important, although I was uncertain exactly why. My attendance at a Catholic church was spotty as I grew up until I essentially stopped going to church in my early teen years. Church seemed completely irrelevant to my life. I considered the Bible an outdated book that was more suitable for old scholars than young simpletons like me. I never stopped believing there was a God, but frankly I had no real idea who God was or how my daily life in any way related to him. I lived as many people do and simply tried to be a moral and spiritual person, hoping that God would think I was a good person who lived a good life.

All of that changed following my graduation from high school. As a graduation present, a young Christian woman I was close to named Grace gave me a very nice leather Bible with my name stamped on the cover in gold lettering. It was the first nice Bible I had ever owned. I thumbed through it a few times during the following summer, but considered it to be more of a good luck charm than a source of instruction.

I was living in a fraternity the first weeks of my freshman year of college when I came to the deep realization that the drunken, girl-crazy frat guy life was not for me. In my heart I truly loved Grace, who was attending another college four hours away. I moved out of the fraternity just before my pledge class was arrested, as God in his providence spared me from participating in the crime and serving jail time by mere days. Unsure of what to do next, I found God calling me to himself through a growing appetite for Scripture. It seemed that nearly all of my classes included pejorative comments and conversations about Christianity, and I decided that I needed to determine for myself what my personal beliefs were about Jesus, Scripture, and Christianity.

I was uncertain which church might be safe to attend, and had heard rumors of some bizarre churches and cults that scared me. So, rather than going to a church or campus ministry, I decided to go to the Bible Grace had bought me. Not knowing where to begin, I just started on the first page, assuming that the Bible was to be read like any other book, from front to back. I started with Genesis, where I expected to see God's people living holy, devout lives that would compel God to love them and would give me an example of how to live a good life.

What I read in Genesis actually shocked me. The book seemed to be mainly about the story of one family that descended from a man named Abraham. While God clearly loved and blessed this family, it was far more like an episode of Jerry Springer than I was expecting. Abraham had both a young wife and an old wife, and pimped out his elderly wife Sarah to some king named Pharaoh to save his own skin. Their grandson Jacob was clearly a con man and ended up marrying two sisters. Later, one of Jacob's sons, Reuben, actually slept with one of his father's wives. The great Noah got drunk and passed out naked in his tent like some redneck on vacation. Some guy named Lot also got drunk, and then his two daughters had sex with him so they could get pregnant. In perhaps the oddest plot twist of all, Judah thought he was picking up a prostitute only to later discover that it was his own daughter-in-law; she had pretended to be a prostitute because she wanted to have his baby, which as far as I could tell must have thrown the entire Hebrew trailer park where Genesis took place into a tizzy.

After Genesis, I continued reading the Old Testament only to find that Moses was known to disobey and argue with God, David was an adulterer and murderer, Solomon had so many women living with him that even Hugh Hefner would have blushed, and other than the occasional person like Joseph, Daniel, or Boaz, most everyone that I had ever heard about in the Old Testament was as messed up as anyone I had ever met.

I finished reading the Old Testament in roughly a month, and although I was enjoying the stories, I was confused about how I should understand them. I had always thought that the Bible was the record of good, moral, religious people and that if I read the Bible I could learn the principles of how to live like them. However, I did not think that having a bunch of wives, sleeping with my mother, impregnating strippers, or being drunk and naked a lot were the application points I was supposed to take from Scripture.

So, I started asking other students who carried Bibles, wore Christian T-shirts, and were open about being Christians about various churches, hoping to find one where I could get some answers about the stuff I had read in the Bible. I had no idea what the differences were between various churches and was afraid of finding myself in one of those places where everyone wears matching white shoes and drinks Kool-Aid in the end. Most of the students said that one church in particular had a nice pastor who did a good job of just teaching the Bible without any weirdness.

I attended that church and was relieved when nothing strange happened, such as someone lying on the platform and twitching like a freshly caught trout or someone passing the plate fifty times asking for more of my money. The pastor, Doug, seemed very normal and humble, and he simply asked us to open our Bibles. His sermon was easy to understand, and he carefully explained each section of a portion of the Bible. After the service I asked one of the students I recognized from a class what the pastor would be teaching on the next Sunday, and she said that he simply taught through books of the Bible, so the following week we'd be in the next section of that Bible book.

I began regularly attending that church and joined some Bible studies led by that pastor. In God's providence, he had a degree in Hebrew from Trinity Evangelical Divinity School and was very well learned in the Old Testament. He patiently explained to me how the Old Testament is about Jesus and how Jesus came to live the sinless life we could not live, die the death for sin we should have died, and rose to give the gift of salvation that we could not earn. As I learned about Jesus from the Old Testament, my desire to know, love, follow, and obey Jesus grew quickly, and I was baptized as a Christian in that church at the age of nineteen. Shortly thereafter, Grace transferred to my college, and we attended Doug's church together and were later married by him when we were twenty-one. The following year we graduated and returned to our hometown of Seattle because God had called us to plant a church there.

At the age of twenty-five we began Mars Hill Church as a small Bible study in our living room. The rest of the story of that church is chronicled in another book I wrote called *Confessions of a Reformission Rev.*,[1] but the basic gist is that the church attracted many young non-Christians who knew very little about Jesus or the Bible, especially the Old Testament. I began meeting with people to answer their questions just as Pastor Doug so graciously had for me. Many people became Christians and were baptized in our small new church. As the church grew from dozens to hundreds and then thousands of people over the years, I could no longer meet with everyone to personally answer their questions. Instead, I began writing booklets that we self-published in our church for people to read. In these little books, I tried to answer the questions I once had and that people I had met with had asked me. Over the years, our church has given away thousands of copies of these booklets for people to read and give to their friends. Upon seeing these brief books, my friends at Crossway asked if they could publish them, which was a humbling encouragement.

1. Driscoll, Mark. *Confessions of a Reformission Rev.: Hard Lessons from an Emerging Missional Church.* Grand Rapids, MI: Zondervan, 2006.

Subsequently, after some editing, these books are now appearing as the series A Book You'll Actually Read. Before we begin answering common questions about the Old Testament, I want to sincerely thank Pastor Doug for being a wonderful first pastor, Grace for buying me my first Bible and being the love of my life and mother of our five children, and the people of Mars Hill Church who have entrusted to me the great honor of teaching them the Bible about Jesus.

1

Answers to Nine Common Questions about the Old Testament

In this chapter I will answer nine of the most common questions I have both had and heard regarding the Old Testament. Before we begin, though, I want to provide some introduction to the Bible, particularly the Old Testament, because I am writing this book with the assumption that many people who read it will do so because, like me, they are hoping to begin with the basics and proceed from there without getting lost in a forest of untaught assumptions, unknown words, and unexplained concepts. Therefore, before we examine the Old Testament in particular, I want to first briefly explain the entire Bible in general.

The New Testament speaks of the Old Testament as Scripture, for which the Greek word is *graphe*, meaning "writing." The word *bible* comes from the Greek word for book. *Holy Bible*, therefore, means "Holy Book."

Our Bible, like history, is divided into the period prior to Jesus' coming (BC or "before Christ") and the period following his coming (AD or *anno Domini*, which is a Latin phrase meaning "in the year of our Lord"). The Bible actually contains sixty-six separate books. Thirty-nine books are in the Old Testament, which is a record of time from God creating the world and our first parents Adam and Eve up until the coming of Jesus Christ into human history. The twenty-seven books of the New Testament begin with the four Gospels, which record the life, death, burial, resurrection, and return to heaven of Jesus, and then proceed to instructions to various

Christians and Christian churches about how to think and live in light of who Jesus is and what he has done. In this way, the Bible is really more of a library of books rather than a single book. However, there is unity and continuity between the various books of the Bible and their Old Testament and New Testament groupings. This point is illustrated by the fact that the New Testament has roughly three hundred explicit Old Testament quotations, as well as upwards of four thousand Old Testament allusions. In many ways, the Old Testament is a series of promises that God makes, and the New Testament is the record of the fulfillment of those promises.

The Bible was originally written over a period of roughly fifteen hundred years by more than forty authors in three languages (the Old Testament in Hebrew, with a bit of Aramaic in Ezra and Daniel, and the New Testament in Greek). Authors of the Old Testament include kings, peasants, philosophers, fishermen, poets, statesmen, scholars, and more. Some books of the Bible clearly state their author (e.g., Josh. 24:26 says that Joshua wrote the book bearing his name). Other books of the Bible do not reveal to us who wrote them (e.g., 1 and 2 Kings). Some books of the Bible are deeply personal, so they require knowledge of the author to be fully appreciated (e.g., Lamentations and Nehemiah 1–7 are essentially journal entries). Meanwhile, other books are historical and literary works that do not necessitate an awareness of who penned them.

Regarding its style, the Bible includes historical records, sermons, letters, a hymnbook, love songs, geographical surveys, architectural specifications, travel diaries, population statistics, family trees, inventories, and numerous legal documents. The Bible is very multicultural, as people from varying continents (Asia, Africa, and Europe), periods of history, backgrounds, incomes, and cultures contributed to the writing of its books.

When first reading through the Old Testament, some people are understandably confused because they simply read through the books of the Bible in the order that they appear, only to find that they are not in chronological order and therefore are difficult to interrelate. This is because our Bible is organized by literary type, much like the books on the shelf at your local library. Therefore, if you would like to read the Old Testament in chronological order, you may want to purchase a chronological Bible so that you can see the timing and relationship between people and events. To help you better understand the books of the Bible according to their literary type, I will later explain each of the Old Testament genres (Pentateuch, history, wisdom, and prophets).

As one reads the Bible, especially the Old Testament, it quickly becomes clear that it includes many records of people, places, and events explained in their historical context. The settings of the Bible range from ancient Egypt under king Pharaoh to Rome under the rule of Augustus. The Bible reveals to us that God is sovereign over history and works in history for individuals, family lines, and nations. What makes the biblical account of history unique is that it does not merely tell us of people, events, and ideas, but it also explains their theological meaning in relation to God. Therefore, the historical record of the Bible is written with the primary purpose of revealing who God is through his work in history so that we can see our lives as inextricably connected to him in every way and only meaningful when understood in light of him.

For these and innumerable other reasons, the Bible is the bestselling book of all time and is available in nearly three thousand languages. However, when you pick up a Bible, while its content will be the same as the ancient version, there are a few differences. The Old Testament was written on papyrus—a form of paper made out of reeds; the New Testament was written on parchments (prepared animal skins). A lecturer at the University of Paris created the Bible's chapter divisions in the early 1200s, which accounts for our current 1,189 chapter divisions. The Bible's 31,173 verse divisions were fully developed by 1551, in an effort to provide addresses (not unlike those on our homes) that would help us find particular sections.

Roughly three-quarters of the Christian Bible is the Old Testament. The Old Testament has 929 chapters and 23,214 verses. The New Testament has 260 chapters and 7,959 verses. In the Old Testament, the longest book is Psalms and the shortest book is Obadiah. In the New Testament, the longest book is Acts and the shortest book is 3 John.

With this brief introduction to the Bible in general, we are prepared to examine the Old Testament in particular. For many, the Old Testament is particularly difficult to comprehend and navigate because of its sheer size and cultural distance from our present age. To make matters worse, theological giants like Martin Luther and John Calvin never produced a single volume dedicated to Old Testament theology. Meanwhile, the majority of Old Testament "scholarship" during the past few hundred years has greatly undermined the message of the Old Testament; such "scholarship" critiques the Old Testament as a very primitive and naïve spirituality that we should evolve beyond, which only further distances Christians from the majority of their Bible.

Some of the devaluation of the Old Testament may be caused by its very title. The term "old" seems to denote information that is archaic, dated, and irrelevant in comparison to the New Testament. It was the early church father Origen (185–254) who first coined the phrases Old and New Testaments. Prior to this designation, the Jews and early church would have only known what we call the Old Testament as the Law, the Prophets, and the Writings, or the Scriptures. Origen's confusion came from misunderstanding Jeremiah's use of the old and new covenants in Jeremiah 31:31. By "new," Jeremiah did not mean something detached from the prior works of God, but something renewed or fulfilled. Therefore, the new covenant is the renewal or fulfillment of the old.

Likewise, the New Testament is inextricably linked to the Old Testament as its renewed fulfillment. By way of example, God's people in the Old Testament received saving grace from God in the same way that Christians in the New Testament do, simply by having faith in God's promises that Jesus would pay the penalty for sin through the cross and empty tomb.[1] In an amazing illustration of just how the New Testament is the renewed fulfillment of the promises of the Old Testament, Paul says that Abraham believed by faith that his seed (Jesus) would save him—and this is the gospel or good news about Jesus Christ that Christians today still trust.[2]

Additionally, the Old Testament was the Bible that Jesus read, believed, and taught because the New Testament had not yet been written. Furthermore, the Bible says that because of studying the Old Testament, "Jesus increased in wisdom and in stature and in favor with God and man."[3]

In the pages of the Bible you will read brutally honest accounts of the pain and joy of human life. Most importantly, you will meet One God who reveals himself as "The LORD, the LORD, a God merciful and gracious, slow to anger, and abounding in steadfast love and faithfulness, keeping steadfast love for thousands, forgiving iniquity and transgression and sin, but who will by no means clear the guilty, visiting the iniquity of the fathers on the children and the children's children, to the third and the fourth generation."[4] It is this Lord, also known as the Lord Jesus Christ, who is the great hero of the Old Testament. It is he who crushes false gods, heals the sick, redeems the enslaved, lifts up the downcast, cares for the poor, disciplines his people, and powerfully rules over human history with a perfect blend of love and justice.

Finally, as we read the Old Testament we must remember that our position in history is not entirely unlike the Old Testament Christians. They read the Old Testament in faith, anticipating the first coming of Jesus to fulfill the promises of the Old Testament. We now read both the Old and New Testaments in faith, eagerly awaiting the second coming of Jesus to fulfill the remaining promises of Scripture given to his people.

1. For example, see Hebrews 11.
2. Gal. 3:8, 14.
3. Luke 2:52.
4. Ex. 34:6–7.

Having examined the Bible in general and the Old Testament in particular, we will now answer the nine most common questions I have had and heard about the Old Testament.

1. Who Wrote the Old Testament?

This question, in many ways, is the most important question we will answer, because how we answer this question in a very real sense determines how we will answer the remaining eight questions. Therefore, it is very important that we consider this question with the utmost seriousness because in it we are determining our personal opinion of the degree to which the Bible is both perfect and authoritative.

On one hand, the Old Testament is written by various human authors, and it clearly tells us who they were. Examples include David writing various psalms,[5] Moses writing all but the closing of the first five books of the Old Testament, also known as the Pentateuch or Law,[6] Joshua writing the book bearing his name,[7] Solomon writing Ecclesiastes,[8] Nehemiah writing the book bearing his name,[9] Daniel writing the book bearing his name,[10] Ezekiel writing the book bearing his name,[11] Jeremiah writing the book bearing his name,[12] Isaiah writing the book bearing his name,[13] and Habakkuk writing the book bearing his name,[14] to only list a few. Other books of

5. For example, Psalms 3:1, 4:1, 5:1, 6:1, 7:1, 8:1, 9:1, and so forth.
6. Ex. 17:14; Deut. 31:24–26.
7. Josh. 24:26.
8. Eccl. 1:1.
9. Neh. 1:1.
10. Dan. 7:1.
11. Ezek. 43:10–11.
12. Jer. 30:2.
13. Isa. 8:1; 30:8.
14. Hab. 2:2.

the Old Testament were spoken by a prophet while a trained scribe wrote down what was said. By way of contemporary analogy, this method is akin to a judge who speaks while presiding over a trial and has a trained stenographer faithfully record every word that he speaks for legal and historical record. For a good example of this kind of Old Testament writing, perhaps the best place to read is Jeremiah 36. Therefore, on one hand the Scripture itself is clear that various human authors were used to record the words that fill the pages of our Bible.

On the other hand, the human authors of Scripture are not the only authors of Scripture. God communicated through the authors of Scripture in a real and miraculous way so that his divine truth could be perfectly communicated through men. The divine and human authorship of Scripture is very much like Jesus himself, who was both fully God and fully man. God the Father chose to work through the humanity of Jesus to reveal himself to us in a manner akin to how he had previously revealed himself to us as God through the men who wrote the Old Testament.

Furthermore, the Old Testament is clear that God spoke through his prophets,[15] and so what the prophet said in God's name was what God said. The Old Testament prophets through whom God gave us the Scriptures state this fact clearly. The phrase "thus says the Lord" is repeated hundreds of times throughout the Old Testament by God's messengers. Other similar statements about prophets speaking by divine authority appear, according to some scholars, as many as 3,800 times throughout the Old Testament. The prophets were well aware that in particular moments of divine revelation given to them by God the Holy Spirit, they were in fact speaking the very words of God himself. In some ways, the prophet was God's megaphone.[16] Therefore, to reject what a prophet had said was to reject what God had commanded.[17]

15. 1 Kings 14:18; 16:12, 34; 2 Kings 9:36; 14:25; Jer. 37:2; Zech. 7:7, 12.
16. 1 Kings 13:21, 26; 21:19; 2 Kings 9:25–26; Hag. 1:12, cf. 1 Sam. 15:3, 18.
17. Deut. 18:19; 1 Sam. 10:8; 13:13–14; 15:3, 19, 23; 1 Kings 20:35, 36.

The belief that God wrote Scripture in concert with human authors whom he inspired to perfectly record his words is called *verbal plenary inspiration*. Very simply, this means that God the Holy Spirit inspired not just the thoughts of Scripture, but also the very details and exact words that were perfectly recorded for us as Scripture. Jesus himself echoed this truth when he said that because God gave us Scripture, it could not be broken.[18]

The Old Testament itself teaches this by stressing how important the exact words of divinely inspired Scripture are:

- "You shall be to me a kingdom of priests and a holy nation. These are the *words* that you shall speak to the people of Israel."[19]
- "Take to heart all the *words* by which I am warning you today, that you may command them to your children, that they may be careful to do all the *words* of this law. For it is no empty *word* for you, but your very life, and by this *word* you shall live long in the land that you are going over the Jordan to possess."[20]
- "Every *word* of God proves true; he is a shield to those who take refuge in him. Do not add to his *words*, lest he rebuke you and you be found a liar."[21]

Furthermore, when the New Testament reflects back upon the Old Testament, it is very clear that Scripture is unlike anything else that has or ever will be written; it alone is divinely inspired by God the Holy Spirit and perfect, despite the fact that it was penned by human authors through whom God chose to speak. The following New

18. Matt. 5:18; Luke 16:17; John 10:35.
19. Ex. 19:6.
20. Deut. 32:46–47.
21. Prov. 30:5–6.

Testament verses are clear examples that this doctrine comes from what Scripture itself plainly states:

- "The prophets who prophesied about the grace that was to be yours searched and inquired carefully, inquiring what person or time the Spirit of Christ in them was indicating when he predicted the sufferings of Christ and the subsequent glories. It was revealed to them that they were serving not themselves but you, in the things that have now been announced to you through those who preached the good news to you by the Holy Spirit sent from heaven, things into which angels long to look."[22]
- "All Scripture is breathed out by God and profitable for teaching, for reproof, for correction, and for training in righteousness, that the man of God may be competent, equipped for every good work."[23]
- "No prophecy of Scripture comes from someone's own interpretation. For no prophecy was ever produced by the will of man, but men spoke from God as they were carried along by the Holy Spirit."[24]

Therefore, the answer to the question, who wrote the Old Testament? is that God wrote the Old Testament through human authors whom God the Holy Spirit inspired to perfectly pen his truth. Subsequently, Christians believe that Scripture is our highest authority, or metaphorical Supreme Court, by which all other lesser authorities are tested. Practically, this means that lesser courts of reason, tradition, and culture are under the highest court of truth, which is divinely inspired Scripture. During the Protestant Reformation, the slogans *sola Scriptura* and *prima Scriptura* became popular

22. 1 Peter 1:10–12.
23. 2 Tim. 3:16–17.
24. 2 Peter 1:20–21.

to summarize this conviction; they mean Scripture alone is our highest authority. This should not be confused with *solo Scriptura*, which is the erroneous belief that truth is only to be found in Scripture and nowhere else. Scripture itself tells us that God reveals truth to us in such things as creation and our conscience, but that the beliefs we may subscribe to from such forms of lesser revelation are to be tested by Scripture. The Old Testament models this for us when it does occasionally quote other books such as the book of Jashar[25] and the Book of the Wars of the Lord.[26] In quoting them, the Bible is not saying that they should be included as sacred Scripture, but rather that they do contain some helpful truth. Practically speaking, this means that a mechanic, doctor, or computer programmer may not consult Leviticus to turn a brake drum, perform open heart surgery, or make an addition to a Linux program, but these experts do possess some helpful truths that, if not forbidden or contradicted by Scripture, are to be gladly received for our benefit.

Having established that Scripture is our highest and most perfect authority and source for truth, we will now examine how the Old Testament speaks of itself.

2. What Does the Old Testament Say about the Old Testament?

The Old Testament often speaks of itself in terms that are both truthfully authoritative and practically helpful. These self-revealing statements are incredibly important because if the Old Testament itself does not say that it is true or helpful, then we have no grounds to claim such things ourselves. The Old Testament does indeed have much to say about itself: it is a perfect guide for our life,[27] altogether pure,[28]

25. Josh. 10:13; 2 Sam. 1:18.
26. Num. 21:14.
27. Prov. 6:23.
28. Pss. 12:6; 119:140.

true,[29] flawless,[30] perfect,[31] wise and practical counsel,[32] effective for God's purposes,[33] precious,[34] and sufficient so that nothing should be taken from or added to it.[35]

The Old Testament also provides richly revealing poetic images that further illuminate its characteristics. God invites our creative imaginations to not merely believe that Scripture is true, but to also meditate on the images through which the Holy Spirit will reveal to us a deeper appreciation for his Word. God does so because he is not only Creator, but also creative, and he created us to appreciate such things as poetry, symbolism, and analogy. The Old Testament is painted as sweetly satisfying like honey,[36] a lamp to guide us along life's often dark path,[37] food that nourishes our soul,[38] and a fire that purifies us and hammer that breaks us so that we can be remade to be increasingly more like Jesus.[39]

Lastly, the Old Testament authors appeal to one another's writings as sacred Scripture. For example, Joshua 1:8 refers to the Pentateuch; Daniel 9:2 refers to Jeremiah; and Ezekiel 14:14 speaks of Noah, Daniel, and Job. Having established what the Old Testament says about itself, we can now add what the New Testament teaches about the Old Testament.

29. Ps. 119:160.
30. Prov. 30:5–6.
31. Ps. 19:7.
32. Prov. 1:1–7; 2:1–22.
33. Isa. 55:11.
34. Ps. 19:10.
35. Deut. 4:2; 12:32.
36. Ps. 119:103.
37. Ps. 119:105.
38. Jer. 15:16.
39. Jer. 23:29.

3. What Does the New Testament Say about the Old Testament?

As mentioned earlier, because the New Testament has roughly three hundred explicit Old Testament quotations, as well as upwards of four thousand Old Testament allusions, it is not surprising to find that the New Testament also has much to say about the Old Testament. These statements can be grouped into three general categories.

First, the New Testament clearly, repeatedly, and emphatically declares that the Old Testament is divinely inspired, sacred Scripture and the very words of God. An entire book could and perhaps should be written on this point, but for the sake of brevity I will simply list many of these instances in a note.[40]

Second, the New Testament makes many statements about the truthfulness and usefulness of the Old Testament. For example, the Old Testament comes with God's power,[41] was written by God's inspiration,[42] is sufficient for all that we truly need to know about God,[43] is true and the source of truth,[44] is for all people regardless of their culture or nation,[45] is necessary to raise children,[46] and ultimately is to be obeyed so that it is not merely a source of information but rather a means of transformation.[47]

Third, like the Old Testament itself, the New Testament uses poetic images to reveal to us how we are to receive the Old Testament. The Old Testament is a sword for battle

40. Matt. 21:42; 22:29; 26:54, 56; Luke 24:25–32, 44–45; John 5:39; 10:35; Acts 17:2, 11; 18:28; Rom. 1:2; 4:3; 9:17; 10:11; 11:2; 15:4; 16:26; 1 Cor. 15:3–4; Gal. 3:8, 22; 4:30; 1 Tim. 5:18; 2 Tim. 3:16; 2 Pet. 1:20–21; 3:15–16.

41. Heb. 4:12.

42. 2 Tim. 3:16; 2 Pet. 1:19–21.

43. Luke 16:29–31.

44. John 17:17.

45. Rom. 16:26.

46. 2 Tim. 3:15.

47. James 1:22.

against Satan, sin, and demons,[48] a seed that God plants in us that grows up as a life of fruitfully faithful living,[49] and milk that nourishes us for life and growth not unlike the feeding of a newborn baby.[50] Having studied what the Old and New Testaments say about the Old Testament, we will now examine what Jesus himself said about it.

4. What Does Jesus Say about the Old Testament?

Jesus summarized the Old Testament Scripture as existing in three parts: the Law, Prophets, and Psalms.[51] He accepted the Old Testament canon as it exists today without any modifications and came to fulfill it.[52] As a rabbi, or preacher and teacher of Scripture, Jesus' entire ministry involved the instruction and application of the Old Testament. Jesus' public ministry even began with him reading from the Old Testament book of Isaiah and stating that his ministry was to fulfill the Old Testament promises about his coming.[53] Jesus clearly stated that his ministry was an Old Testament ministry in that it was to fulfill all of the Old Testament promises and longings that pointed to him.

Consequently, it is impossible to be a faithful Christian and not fully embrace the Old Testament as God's Word. Occasionally, someone will claim to be a Christian yet not embrace all of the Old Testament. One example is an ancient heretic (false teacher) named Marcion. He said that the Old Testament was in fact a far lesser book than the New Testament and encouraged Christians to remove it from their Bible.

48. Eph. 6:17; Heb. 4:12.
49. James 1:21.
50. 1 Pet. 2:2.
51. Luke 24:44.
52. Matt. 5:17.
53. Luke 4:16–21.

Unlike Marcion, however, Jesus clearly accepted and taught the Old Testament as sacred Scripture without reservation. Subsequently, we must either accept Rabbi Jesus as our most trustworthy Old Testament teacher or confess that he was a poor Bible teacher who made errors—and in turn elevate some other teacher over him that we trust more fully. I am refuting the seemingly endless parade of Bible "scholars" who somehow simultaneously claim to be faithful Christian Bible teachers while disagreeing with the teaching of The Bible Teacher, Jesus Christ. Without seeming too negative on this point, I must say that this is a constant issue with the college students who attend our church. Many of them take classes on the Bible at both public and private colleges taught by professors who claim to be Christians. Yet, many of these professors belittle their Christian students for simply believing the Scriptures. These students often speak to me about their confusion, asking what they should do. I share the following points with them and tell them to humbly defend the teachings of Jesus, even if it should result in scorn and getting a lower grade, because Jesus himself was poorly treated by the self-appointed "scholars" in his own day who were too arrogant to see that there is no Bible scholar greater than Jesus.

First, the parts of the Old Testament that are most commonly rejected as erroneous are also those sections of Scripture that Jesus clearly taught. This includes the literalness of Genesis 1 and 2,[54] Cain and the murder of Abel,[55] Noah and the flood,[56] Abraham,[57] Sodom and Gomorrah,[58] Lot,[59] Isaac and Jacob,[60] the manna,[61] the wil-

54. Matt. 19:4–5; Mark 10:6–8.
55. Matt. 23:35; Luke 11:51.
56. Matt. 24:37–39; Luke 17:26–27.
57. John 8:56.
58. Matt. 10:15; 11:23–24; Luke 10:12; 17:29.
59. Luke 17:28–32.
60. Matt. 8:11; Luke 13:28.
61. John 6:31, 49, 58.

derness serpent,[62] Moses as lawgiver,[63] the popularity of the false prophets,[64] and Jonah in the belly of a great fish.[65]

Second, in matters of controversy, Jesus used the Old Testament as his court of appeals.[66] On many occasions when an Old Testament teaching was questioned, Jesus simply believed the clear teaching of Old Testament Scripture and defended himself by saying, "It is written."[67]

Third, in times of crisis, Jesus quoted from the Old Testament, indicating that it was his source of truth, solace, and defense. For example, when tempted by Satan, Jesus quoted from the book of Deuteronomy.[68] At the moment of his death, Jesus quoted Psalm 22:1: "My God, my God, why have you forsaken me?"[69] And breathing his last in Luke 23:46, Jesus quoted Psalm 31:5, saying, "Into your hands I commit my spirit."

Fourth, Jesus repeatedly taught that Old Testament prophecy had been fulfilled.[70]

Fifth, Jesus named the authors of some Old Testament books. Some of the most common critiques launched at the Old Testament are in regard to authorship. For example, many Old Testament "scholars" boldly claim that Moses did not pen any of the first five books of the Old Testament, or that two or three authors penned

62. John 3:14.

63. Matt. 8:4; 19:8; Mark 1:44; 7:10; 10:5; 12:26; Luke 5:14; 20:37; John 5:46; 7:19.

64. Luke 6:26.

65. Matt. 12:40.

66. Matt. 5:17–20; 22:29; 23:23; Mark 12:24.

67. Matt. 4:4, 6, 10; 11:10; 21:13; 26:24, 31; Mark 1:2; 7:6; 9:12ff.; 11:17; 14:21, 27; Luke 2:23; 4:4, 8, 10, 17; 7:27; 10:26; 19:46; 22:37; John 2:17; 6:31, 45; 8:17; 10:34.

68. Matt. 4:1–11, cf. Deut. 8:3; 6:13, 16.

69. Matt. 27:46; Mark 15:34.

70. Matt. 11:10, cf. Luke 7:27; Matt. 26:24; Matt. 26:31, cf. Mark 14:27; Matt. 26:53–56, cf. Mark 14:49; Mark 9:12–13; 14:21; Luke 4:21; 18:31–33; 21:22; 22:37; 24:25–27; 24:44–47; John 5:39–47; John 13:18, cf. Ps. 41:9; John 15:25, cf. Ps. 35:19; John 17:12.

Isaiah—none of whom was actually Isaiah. But Jesus taught that Scripture was authored by Moses,[71] Isaiah,[72] David,[73] and Daniel.[74] Therefore, we are again left with the simple decision of whether we will accept Jesus as the most accurate and trustworthy Old Testament teacher or replace him with another teacher or school of thought that we consider to have greater integrity and insight.

In summary, Jesus taught that the Old Testament was perfectly inspired and totally truthful Scripture. Jesus devoted his ministry to teaching the Old Testament, defending the Old Testament, fulfilling the Old Testament, and using the Old Testament. Having established the authorship of the Old Testament and reflected upon what the Old Testament, New Testament, and Jesus have to say about the Old Testament, we will now examine how its thirty-nine books were chosen to be in the Bible.

5. How Were the Old Testament Books Chosen as Scripture?

Canonization is the process by which some books were included in the Old Testament while others were excluded. *Canon* is a word meaning "a measuring rod." The canon is the standard that all scriptural books must meet. The books of the Bible were authoritative, and the Old Testament books shared the following five particular traits that distinguished them from other mere books:

1. They were written by a prophet of God.[75]
2. That prophet's authority was confirmed by an act of God.[76]

71. Mark 7:10.
72. Mark 7:6; Matt. 13:14.
73. Mark 12:36.
74. Matt. 24:15.
75. Deut. 18:18–22; 1 Pet. 1:20–21.
76. Heb. 2:3–4.

3. The prophetic writings told the truth about God in harmony with God's other prophets.[77]
4. The prophetic writings were accompanied with the power of God to change people's lives.[78]
5. The prophetic writings were accepted by the people of God as true.[79]

There is little if any dispute about the books of the Old Testament. God's people in the Old Testament quickly accepted those books as inspired by God.

When an Old Testament prophet spoke, it was clear that God had spoken. For example, the tablets of the Law were preserved in the Ark, which was the place of God's presence on the earth. This placement indicates the sanctity with which they were considered.[80] The Five Books of Moses (also called the Pentateuch, which means "one book in five parts") were placed alongside them as soon as Moses wrote them.[81] The writings of the other prophets were added.[82] The Scriptures were eventually moved to the temple to be cared for by the priests in the days of Solomon.[83]

To this very day, Jews continue to have the same exact books as their Bible. The "Hebrew Bible" of Judaism is virtually identical to the Christian Old Testament, with a few organizational exceptions. For example, their books are in a different order than the Christian Bible, and sometimes they combine two books into one, such as Ezra–Nehemiah.

77. Deut. 13:1–5; 18:22; Gal. 1:8.

78. Heb. 4:12.

79. Deut. 31:24–26; Josh. 24:26; 1 Sam. 10:25; Dan. 9:2; Col. 4:16; 1 Thess. 2:13; 5:27; 1 Tim. 5:18; 2 Pet. 3:16.

80. Ex. 25:16–21; 40:20; Deut. 10:5; 1 Kings 8:9.

81. Deut. 31:24–26.

82. 1 Sam. 10:25; Josh. 24:25–26; Isa. 8:20; 29:18; 34:16.

83. 1 Kings 8:6–9; 2 Kings 22:8.

Nonetheless, Jews and Christians agree that the content of the Old Testament as we have it is the total canon of Scripture before the time of Jesus. Jesus himself agrees with this. By the time of his birth, the content of the Old Testament was a settled matter, and Jesus accepted, learned, and taught the Old Testament as we have it without modification.

Furthermore, Jesus summarized the Bible as existing in three parts: the Law, Prophets, and Psalms.[84] Jesus also spoke of the Old Testament as existing from Abel (from Genesis, the first book of the Old Testament) to Zechariah (a contemporary of Malachi, the final book of the Old Testament).[85]

The Hebrew canon was closed and settled with the final book of the Old Testament, Malachi, around 400 BC. Malachi concluded with the promise that the next event in redemptive history would be the coming of John the Baptist, who would prepare the way for Jesus, and Jesus would come to the temple.[86] Importantly, the temple was destroyed in AD 70, which means that the Jews who are still waiting for a Messiah today wait in vain because Jesus was that Messiah and after AD 70 the promise of Malachi could not be fulfilled.

During the four hundred years of silence between the end of the Old Testament and the coming of Jesus, many other works were written, including books of history, fiction, practical living, and end-times speculation. These books are also known as the *apocrypha*, which means "hidden" or "secret" because the religious leaders of that time preferred that the books not be widely read by the people.

While these books were read by some of God's people, they were treated like popular Christian books in our own day, such as those by C. S. Lewis; they were

84. Luke 24:44.
85. Matt. 23:35; Luke 11:51.
86. Mal. 3:1; 4:5–6, cf. Matt. 3:1–17; 17:9–13; Luke 1:16–17; 3:1–18.

never accepted as Scripture, for many reasons. First, many of the apocryphal books were also *pseudepigraphal*, meaning that they were written under a pen name so that the true identity of the author would be unknown. The pen names were often those of biblical people (e.g., Enoch, Abraham, Moses, Solomon), deceitfully leading readers to believe the books were written by these biblical men. It would be similar to me putting Billy Graham's name on this book to sell more copies. Second, while the Old Testament is quoted roughly three hundred times in the New Testament, none of the apocryphal books are ever quoted in the New Testament or even alluded to, with the exception of a very debated section of Jude. Third, both Jews and Christians rejected any of the apocryphal books as divinely inspired sacred Scripture until the Catholic Council of Trent in 1546. At that time, the Catholic Church was facing a growing protest movement (now known as Protestantism) that denounced some of the church's teaching as unbiblical. Among the chief critics was the Catholic monk Martin Luther, who pointed out that praying to saints, paying indulgences to the church, and purgatory were not found in the Bible. In an effort to defend themselves, the Catholic Church voted to insert new books into the Bible, more than a millennium after the Old Testament canon had been closed and the apocryphal books had been rejected as Scripture. Why? Because it found some support for its unbiblical doctrines in the apocrypha and, rather than changing its doctrines, it instead chose to change its Bible. Subsequently, if you open Catholic—and even some Orthodox—Bibles today, you will find books with names such as Tobit, Judith, the Wisdom of Solomon, Ecclesiasticus or the Wisdom of Jesus ben Sirach, Baruch, 1 Maccabees, and 2 Maccabees, as well as additions to Esther and the book of Daniel (such as the Prayer of Azariah or the Song of the Three Young Men, Susanna, and Bel and the Dragon).

I am not trying to be mean-spirited to or disparaging of Catholics. I was raised in a Catholic family, attended a Catholic school for three years, and as a young boy even assisted the priest with Mass by serving as an altar boy. Many of my relatives are

Chart 1.1 *A Summarized Historical Timeline of Scripture*

Old Testament (1800–400 BC)	Intertestamental Period (400 Silent Years)	Life of Jesus (roughly 0–AD 33)
• Prophets spoke, "Thus says the Lord." • Some prophets wrote their books (Jer. 36; Josh. 24:26; Isa. 30:8; Ezek. 43:11; Hab. 2:2; Dan. 7:1–2; 2 Chron. 21:12). • Some prophets had a scribe (Ex. 17:14; 34:28). • Books were treated as sacred: • Placed in ark (Deut. 31:24–26). • Placed in sanctuary (Josh. 24:26). • Placed before God (1 Sam. 10:25). • Books showed the power of God changing peoples' lives (2 Kings 22–23; Ex. 24:7; Neh. 8). • Old Testament books appeal to each other for authority as God's Word: • Joshua 1:8 refers to the Pentateuch. • Daniel 9:2 refers to Jeremiah. • Ezekiel 14:14 refers to Noah, Daniel, and Job. • Old Testament ends with the last prophet Malachi: • Promises that the next event will be Jesus coming to the Temple (Mal. 3:1). • Promises that the next prophet will be John the Baptizer (Mal. 4:4–6).	• No new books of Scripture are given. • The Old Testament canon is settled without any significant debates regarding certain books. • Apocryphal ("hidden") books are written as history, fiction, wisdom, and apocalyptic literature that become popular books but are never considered to be Scripture.	• Four hundred silent years end with John the Baptizer and Jesus (Matt. 3:1–17; 17:9–13; Luke 1:8–17).

New Testament (AD 45–95)	Pseudepigrapha
• Jesus spoke of Old Testament history as existing from Abel (Genesis) to Zechariah (the time of Malachi) (Matt. 23:35; Luke 11:51).	• Authors under pen names pretend to be eyewitnesses to Jesus and write various false gospels (e.g., the Gospel of Thomas).
• Jesus described the Old Testament as Law, Prophets, and Psalms (Luke 24:44).	
• Jesus quoted the Old Testament freely for teaching.	
• Jesus and the New Testament writers never quote any apocryphal books. They accepted the Old Testament as we have it.	
• Jesus promised the Holy Spirit would inspire his disciples (John 14:26; 16:13).	
• New Testament writers were nearly all eyewitnesses (e.g., 1 John 1:1–3).	
• New Testament books claim to be Scripture (1 Cor. 14:37; 1 Thess. 2:13; 2 Thess. 2:15; Col 4:16; Rev. 1:3).	
• New Testament authors claim works of other disciples were Scripture (2 Pet. 3:15–16).	
• After all eyewitnesses died, some pseudepigraphal (pen named) books were written by people pretending to be apostles.	
• Almost all New Testament books were accepted by the second century, and all were finalized by the fourth century.	
• No apocryphal books were accepted until the Catholic Council of Trent in 1546.	

Catholic, and I have some dear friends and relatives who are Christian Catholics who love Jesus and will be with me in heaven forever. However, on this point of what books belong in the Old Testament, I disagree with my Catholic friends. To be honest, I have seen the Catholic Church make some changes to its doctrines in recent years in an effort to be more aligned with what Scripture teaches, which is encouraging. Yet there is no more reason to support the politically motivated insertion of apocryphal books into the Bible over fifteen hundred years after they were written and rejected than there is to decide today to include a new list of ancient books that do not claim to be inspired as part of the New Testament Scriptures.

In an effort to summarize much of what I have tried to explain thus far, I have condensed the main points into chart 1.1 as a historical timeline of the writing of Scripture.

6. What Is the Central Message of the Old Testament?

We will now explore how the Old Testament is to be rightly understood in light of its central message. The opening line of Scripture introduces us to its hero, God. Throughout the pages of Scripture this God is revealed. In the closing line of the New Testament Scriptures, we are reminded that the God who is the hero of the true story of Scripture is Jesus Christ. Thus, the written Word of God reveals to us the incarnate ("in human flesh") Word of God, Jesus Christ. Further, without the written Word we cannot rightly know of the incarnate Word. Therefore, defining the central message of the Old Testament is the key to our interpretive process because without a proper understanding of Scripture we do not have access to truly loving and knowing the real Jesus.

Some people prefer the New Testament to the Old Testament because they wrongly believe that only the New Testament is about Jesus. However, it was Jesus himself who taught that the Old Testament was primarily about him. While arguing with the "theologians" in his day, Jesus chastised them, saying, "You search the Scriptures [Old Testament] because you think that in them you have eternal life; and it is they that bear witness about me, yet you refuse to come to me that you may have life."[87]

Following his resurrection, Jesus opened the Old Testament to teach others about himself: "Beginning with Moses and all the Prophets, he interpreted to them in all the Scriptures the things concerning himself."[88] Likewise, in speaking to his disciples, Jesus said, "These are my words that I spoke to you while I was still with you, that everything written about me in the Law of Moses and the Prophets and the Psalms must be fulfilled."[89] We then read that he "opened their minds to understand the Scriptures."[90]

Jesus' own words about himself as the central message of the Old Testament are pointedly clear. He said, "Do not think that I have come to abolish the Law or the Prophets; I have not come to abolish them but to fulfill them. For truly, I say to you, until heaven and earth pass away, not an iota, not a dot, will pass from the Law until all is accomplished."[91]

To emphasize this point, we will examine only a few of the many examples taken from Jesus' life where he was acutely aware that his acts were fulfilling the promises of the Old Testament. After reading from the scroll of Isaiah in the synagogue early in his ministry, "he rolled up the scroll and gave it back to the attendant and sat down. And the eyes of all in the synagogue were fixed on him. And he began to say to them, 'Today this Scripture has been fulfilled in your hearing.'"[92] At the last supper, on the

87. John 5:39–40.
88. Luke 24:27.
89. Luke 24:44.
90. Luke 24:45.
91. Matt. 5:17–18.
92. Luke 4:20–21.

night before his betrayal, Jesus taught about his impending death from Isaiah 53:12 by saying, "For I tell you that this Scripture must be fulfilled in me: 'And he was numbered with the transgressors.' For what is written about me has its fulfillment."[93] Upon his betrayal by Judas and his arrest, Jesus said, "But all this has taken place that the Scriptures of the prophets might be fulfilled."[94] Clearly, Jesus saw himself and his ministry as the very fulfillment of the Old Testament promises.

Simply, when the Old Testament is rightly interpreted, it is ultimately about Jesus as God, our Savior, the object of our faith, forgiver of our sins, and giver of eternal life. Therefore, to correctly interpret the Old Testament you will need to connect its verses, concepts, and events to Jesus.

Prophetic Promises

The Old Testament uses various means to reveal Jesus, including promises, appearances, types, and titles. First, the Old Testament teaches about Jesus in the numerous prophetic promises given about him. At the time of its writing, upwards of one-quarter of Scripture was prophetic in nature, promising future events. Neither Islam nor any other world religion or cult can present any specific prophecies concerning the coming of their prophets. However, in the Old Testament we see hundreds of fulfilled prophecies extending hundreds and sometimes over a thousand years into the future. Consider the following Old Testament prophecies and their fulfillment in Jesus Christ:

- Seven hundred years before the birth of Jesus, Isaiah promised that Jesus' mother would be a virgin who would conceive by a miracle.[95]

93. Luke 22:37.
94. Matt. 26:56.
95. Isa. 7:14; Matt. 1:18–23.

- Seven hundred years before the birth of Jesus, Micah promised that Jesus would be born in Bethlehem.[96]
- Seven hundred years before the birth of Jesus, Hosea promised that Jesus' family would flee as refugees to Egypt to save his young life.[97]
- Four hundred years before the birth of Jesus, Malachi promised that Jesus would enter the temple. Since the temple was destroyed in AD 70, this prophecy could not be fulfilled anytime after AD 70.[98]
- Five hundred years before the birth of Jesus, Zechariah promised that Jesus would be betrayed for thirty pieces of silver.[99]
- One thousand years before the birth of Jesus, David promised that lots would be cast for Jesus' clothing.[100]
- One thousand years before the birth of Jesus (and hundreds of years before the invention of crucifixion), David promised that Jesus would be crucified.[101]
- Seven hundred years before the birth of Jesus, Isaiah promised that Jesus would die and be buried in a rich man's tomb.[102]
- One thousand years before the birth of Jesus, David promised that Jesus would resurrect from death;[103] seven hundred years before the birth of Jesus, Isaiah also promised that Jesus would resurrect from death.[104]

96. Mic. 5:2; Luke 2:1–7.
97. Hos. 11:1; Matt. 2:13–15.
98. Mal. 3:1; Luke 2:25–27.
99. Zech. 11:12–13; Matt. 26:14–15.
100. Ps. 22:18; John 19:23–24.
101. Ps. 22:16; Luke 23:33.
102. Isa. 53:8–9; Matt. 27:57–60; Luke 23:46.
103. Ps. 16:10.
104. Isa. 53:10–12; Acts 2:25–32.

The fulfillments of these prophetic promises show the divine inspiration of Scripture and prove that there is a sovereign God who rules over human history and brings events to pass just as he ordains them. Because of these facts, we can trust the internal consistency of the Bible to be a chorus of faithful witnesses who sing together in harmony about the glory of Jesus Christ.

Christophonies

Second, the Old Testament teaches about Jesus through appearances that he makes before his birth, or what are called *Christophonies*. Examples include walking with Abraham,[105] wrestling with Jacob,[106] appearing to Moses,[107] joining Daniel in the fiery furnace,[108] and calling Isaiah into ministry.[109] Other examples may include the occasional appearance of "the angel [messenger] of the Lord" who is sometimes identified as God.[110] This angel provided the sacrifice in Isaac's place[111] and spoke and journeyed with Moses.[112]

Types

Third, *types* are Old Testament representative figures, institutions, or events that foreshadow Jesus. Examples include Adam, who foreshadows Jesus as the second Adam; the priesthood, which prefigures Jesus as our High Priest; David and other kings, who prefigure Jesus as the King of Kings; Moses and the prophets, who pre-

105. Genesis 18, cf. John 8:56.
106. Gen. 32:30.
107. Ex. 3:2–6, cf. John 8:58.
108. Dan. 3:24–25.
109. Isa. 6:1–5, cf. John 12:41.
110. Judg. 6:11–14; 13:22.
111. Gen. 16:7–13.
112. Ex. 3:14; 23:20–21, cf. John 8:56–59.

figure Jesus as our ultimate Prophet; animal sacrifices, which prefigure Jesus as the sinless Lamb of God slain for our sins; the temple, which prefigures God's presence dwelling among us in Jesus; shepherds who care for their sheep, which remind us we are as foolish and vulnerable as sheep but that Jesus our Shepherd keeps constant watch over us; judges, who foreshadow Jesus as the final judge of all people; and many others.

We also see people in the Old Testament who perform various kinds of service analogous to the services that Jesus performs perfectly. Unlike the first Adam, Jesus Christ is the Last Adam who passed his test in a garden and in so doing imputed his righteousness to us to overcome the sin imputed to us through the sin of the first Adam. Jesus is the true and better Abel who, although he was innocent, was slain and whose blood cries out for our acquittal. When Abraham left his father and home, he was doing the same thing that Jesus would do when he left heaven. When Isaac carried his own wood and laid down his life to be sacrificed at the hand of his father Abraham, he was showing us what Jesus would later do. Jesus is the greater Jacob, who wrestled with God in Gethsemane and, though wounded and limping, walked away from his grave blessed. Jesus is the greater Joseph who serves at the right hand of God the King, extends forgiveness and provision to those of us who have betrayed him, and uses his power to save us in loving reconciliation. Jesus is greater than Moses in that he stands as a mediator between God and us, bringing us the New Covenant. Like Job, innocent Jesus suffered and was tormented by the Devil so that God might be glorified, while his dumb friends were no help or encouragement. Jesus is a King greater than David, who has slain our giants of Satan, sin, and death, although in the eyes of the world he was certain to face a crushing defeat at their hands. Jesus is greater than Jonah in that he spent three days in the grave and not just a fish to save a multitude even greater than Nineveh.

Furthermore, when Boaz redeemed Ruth and brought her and her despised people into community with God's people, he was showing what Jesus would do to redeem his bride the church from all the nations of the earth. When Nehemiah rebuilt Jerusalem, he was doing something similar to Jesus, who is building for us a New Jerusalem as our eternal home. When Hosea married an unfaithful whoring wife whom he continued to pursue in love, he was showing us the heart of Jesus, who does the same for his unfaithful bride, the church. Finally, when God's people sought to keep their homes free from filth through various Old Testament rituals, they were showing that their lives were filled with the filth of sin and they desperately needed Jesus to come and make them clean.

We also see Jesus in the Old Testament through various events. For example, in the Exodus account of Passover, Moses met with the elders of Israel to instruct all the people to follow the Lord's commands for the Passover Feast. They were to place blood over their doorframes with hyssop (a common herb bundled for cleaning), and no one was to leave home until the morning. By being marked with a lamb's blood, death would not come to the home but would pass over. Paul says that we see Jesus in this because "we have now been justified by his [Jesus'] blood, much more shall we be saved by him [Jesus] from the wrath of God."[113] Peter also says our salvation is given by Jesus Christ and "sprinkling with his blood."[114]

Likewise, the exodus serves as the pattern of our own salvation: Jesus crushed Satan like he did Pharaoh and liberated us into freedom that we might worship him like the Israelites did. The meaning of the crucifixion of Jesus was revealed in the annual celebration of Yom Kippur or the Day of Atonement. This was the most important day of the year. It was intended to deal with the sin problem between humanity

113. Rom. 5:9.
114. 1 Pet. 1:2.

and God. On that day, two healthy goats without defect were chosen to represent sinless perfection. The high priest would slaughter one goat, which acted as a substitute for the sinners who rightly deserved a violently bloody death for their many sins. This goat's blood was shed as a price for sin, showing us how Jesus would die in our place for our sins. The second goat was allowed to run free with its sins forgiven, showing us how Jesus would not only die for our sins but also take them away.

Titles

Fourth, there are many titles for God in the Old Testament that refer to Jesus Christ as God. In Daniel 7:13–14, God is called the "son of man," and Jesus adopted that as his favorite title, using it some eighty times in the four Gospels. Jesus is the Suffering Servant that was promised in Isaiah.[115] Jesus is also known by many other Old Testament titles for God, including First and Last,[116] Light,[117] Rock,[118] Husband or Bridegroom,[119] Shepherd,[120] Redeemer,[121] Savior,[122] and the Lord of Glory.[123]

Much more could be said, but all of these examples illustrate the one big idea that Jesus is the central theme of the entire Old Testament. To properly understand the Old Testament we must connect it to the person and work of Jesus. This should not be done in an allegorizing manner where arbitrary meanings foreign to Scripture are

115. Isa. 42:1–4, 49:1–7, 52:13–53:12, cf. Phil. 2:1–11.
116. Isa. 41:4, 44:6, 48:12, cf. Rev. 1:17, 2:8, 22:13.
117. Ps. 27:1, cf. John 1:9.
118. Pss. 18:2, 95:1, cf. 1 Cor. 10:4, 1 Pet. 2:6–8.
119. Hos. 2:16; Isa. 62:5, cf. Eph. 5:28–33, Rev. 21:2.
120. Ps. 23:1, cf. Heb. 13:20.
121. Hos. 13:14, Ps. 130:7, cf. Titus 2:13, Rev. 5:9.
122. Isa. 43:3, cf. John 4:42.
123. Isa. 42:8, cf. 1 Cor. 2:8.

assigned to Old Testament words and images, thereby changing their meaning. Rather, the message of the Old Testament includes symbolism and identity that are most fully revealed in Jesus.

It is my desire that you really embrace this simple but transforming truth. Unless Jesus is the central message of the Old Testament, many errors abound. The most common is moralizing. Moralizing is reading the Old Testament not to learn about Jesus, but only to learn principles for how to live my life as a good person by following the good examples of some people and avoiding the bad examples of others. That kind of approach to the Old Testament is not Christian because it is not about Christ. It treats the Bible like any other book with moral lessons that are utterly disconnected from the example and empowerment of Jesus.

Therefore, the issue of Jesus is the difference between how Christians and adherents of other religions (e.g., Jews and Muslims) understand the Old Testament. This point was made painfully clear to me one day while driving home from the church that I pastor. I had just finished a sermon from Genesis when I heard an advertisement on Christian radio. A group of churches in our region were getting together for a conference on understanding the message of the Old Testament. I was glad to hear that . . . until I heard the rest of the details. The Christian churches were bringing in a non-Christian rabbi who did not believe in Jesus to teach all the Christians how to study the Old Testament. My heart was absolutely broken because I knew he would not tell them anything about Jesus and in so doing would only be able to moralize. The sad result of moralizing is that people become proud like Satan if they think they are obeying the moral commands of Scripture, or depressed if they are honest enough to admit their sinful shortcomings. God's intention for our study of the Old Testament is never demonic pride or hopeless despair, but rather Jesus Christ—who not only shows us how to live but transforms us so that we can.

7. How Did We Get the Old Testament in English?

Now that we have learned that the Old Testament was primarily written in Hebrew to Hebrews and fulfilled by the Hebrew Jesus, you may be wondering how it came to pass that the Hebrew Bible was translated into English. Many volumes have been written to explain the miraculous and fascinating process necessary for the Bible's existence. The following five-step sequence is a simple way to explain this process.

God → Revelation/Inspiration → Transmission → Translation → Interpretation → Application → Your Life

Revelation is the miraculous event whereby God revealed himself and his Truth to certain people and inspired them, through the power of the Holy Spirit, to write down what he had to say—perfectly. The original copy is called the *autographa*. The Old Testament autographa was stored in the temple in the days of Solomon until Jerusalem was destroyed in the sixth century BC. At that time, the autographa was either destroyed or scattered. Later, Ezra and other religious leaders collected the remaining manuscripts of the Old Testament books and compiled them as one collection and stored them in an ark made for the second temple.

Transmission occurred when the autographa was carefully copied by trained scribes so that other copies could be made available for people to read. This process was painstaking and was the only means by which any ancient document could be reproduced until the invention of the printing press in the fifteenth century AD.

Today some Jewish scribes continue the process of transmission much like their ancient counterparts. They arise early in the morning, undergo ritual bathing, spend time praying and reciting religious texts, and then write letter by letter as another scribe reads a manuscript aloud. The entire process is carefully undertaken, religiously devoted, and a great insight into how the process occurred in the past.

While the handwritten copies had the occasional minor error (e.g., spelling or punctuation), the existence of multiple copies allowed the scribes to determine which scrolls had mistakes. For example, if two hundred scrolls spelled a word one way and two scrolls spelled it another way, it was evident which scrolls were actually in error. Thus, the copied scrolls were accepted as accurate and authoritative by God's people in the Old Testament.[124] Also, the apostles, who were the senior leaders in the early church, taught from copies of the Old Testament books of the Bible.[125] The early church tested all teachings against the existing Old Testament scrolls.[126] Furthermore, Jesus himself taught from copies of the Old Testament books, not the autographa, and treated them as authoritative.[127] In conclusion, God's people have always relied on manuscripts, and these writings have proven to be accurate and trustworthy. Jesus' own perfect example assures us of their trustworthiness. In addition, we trust this same process when reading every other ancient document because we do not usually have access to their original copies either, but have depended on copies for our modern translations.

The copies of Old Testament manuscripts we possess today generally fall into three categories. The largest grouping is the Masoretic texts, with the earliest copies dating anywhere from AD 600 to AD 1000. The second category is the Dead Sea Scrolls. These scrolls are some of the most important findings in the history of biblical literature. In 1947, a shepherd boy stumbled across jars of scrolls in some caves while searching for a lost goat. The age and quality of many of the scrolls was unprecedented, with some dating as far back as 400 BC, which was as many as one thousand years

124. Deut. 17:18, cf. 1 Kings 2:3; Ezra 7:14; Neh. 8:8.
125. Acts 17:2; 18:8.
126. Acts 17:11.
127. Matt. 12:3–5; 21:16, 42; Luke 4:16–21; 10:26.

earlier than any previously discovered scroll. My family and I had the privilege of seeing some of these scrolls and fragments of scrolls on display in Seattle as part of a traveling exhibit that gives tremendous instruction on the entire process of transmitting the Old Testament. The Hebrew manuscripts of the Torah (the first five books of the Old Testament) that were preserved in Samaritan non-Jewish communities make up the final grouping of Old Testament manuscripts from which various translations are drawn.

Translation occurs in service to people who want to read the books of the Bible but are not familiar with the original languages in which they were written (Hebrew, Greek, and Aramaic). Teams of language theory scholars carefully undertake the painstaking process of translating the original languages into the languages of other peoples.

Two of the most important early translations of the Old Testament were the Septuagint and the Vulgate, which translated the original Hebrew into Greek and then Latin when they became the primary languages of the Western world. Today, the Bible has been carefully translated into nearly three thousand languages. John Wycliffe initiated the first translation of the English Bible (from Latin), and John Purvey completed it in AD 1388. William Tyndale, who was educated at Oxford and Cambridge, translated the first English Bible from the original Hebrew and Greek.

While the thought of a translation may concern some people, the fact remains that most of the canon of Western literature has also been translated because we do not use their original languages, either.

Interpretation occurs when someone reads the Bible in a language they can understand and determines the meaning of the verses they read by the enablement of God the Holy Spirit who also inspired the writing of Scripture. Each text of the Bible has only one true interpretation, and so we must be careful to read the truth out of the Bible (*exegesis*) rather than reading our beliefs and desires into it (*eisegesis*).

A common question arises at this point: is the Bible to be interpreted literally? The answer is yes. There are plain-literal and figurative-literal portions of the Bible. When interpreting Scripture, we begin by assuming the plain-literal meaning, and if that seems absurd then we go with a figurative-literal interpretation. A figurative-literal Scripture teaches a truth in a poetic way and often uses the words "like" or "as" to tip us off that figurative language is being used. But even when figurative language is being used, it is still communicating a literal truth. For example, in the poetic Song of Songs, the man says to his beloved, "your eyes are doves."[128] In this figurative language, the man is communicating a very literal truth. He likens her eyes to doves, which come in pairs, and when their tail-feathers flutter they appear like eyelashes. Doves have just one faithful mate throughout their lives, possibly indicating that her eyes are focused on him alone. The dove is also a symbol of peace and purity, alluding to her virginity.

I have also been asked many times whether we need to obey all commands in the Old Testament. The short answer regarding law is that all of the Old Testament commands/laws were fulfilled in Jesus Christ.[129] This does not mean that we do not love and value the Old Testament law. But it does mean that we are no longer under it. Similarly, when I was in high school I had to sign an attendance sheet every day, go to assemblies, and bring a note if I had been sick. Since the graduation requirements have been met, I am no longer bound to do those things. This does not mean they were bad, only that they are completed. However, there are some laws from high school that are still binding on me. For example, at my school I was not allowed to

128. Song 1:15.
129. Matt. 5:17–18.

kill anyone, sell drugs, or steal. These laws are still applicable to me, even though I have graduated.

Likewise, there are three kinds of laws in the Old Testament. First, there are ceremonial laws, which are related to the priesthood, sacrifices, temple, and cleanness. These are now fulfilled in Jesus (for example, nearly the entire book of Hebrews addresses this issue for Jews who struggled with the Old Testament laws once they were saved). These laws are no longer binding on us because Jesus is our priest, sacrifice, temple, and cleanser. Second, there are civil laws, which refer to the governing of Israel as a nation ruled by God. Since we are no longer a theocracy, these laws, while insightful, are not directly binding on us. As Romans 13 says, we must now obey our pagan government because God will work through it, too. Third, there are moral laws, which prohibit such things as stealing, murdering, and lying. These laws are still binding on us even though Jesus fulfilled their requirements through his sinless life. Jesus himself repeats and reinforces nine of the Ten Commandments. The only exception is the Sabbath, because that is part of the ceremonial law. Now our rest is in the finished work of Jesus, not just a day. In summary, the ceremonial and civil laws of the Old Testament are no longer binding on us, while the moral laws are.

Application means taking what we learn from the principles in the Bible and making changes in our thoughts and actions by God the Holy Spirit's empowering grace so that our life is congruent with the Bible. There are a seemingly infinite number of applications for a text of the Bible. For example, when the Bible says that we should love people, the applications for that principle are endless.

In this five-step process (Revelation/Inspiration → Transmission → Translation → Interpretation → Application), we see how God speaks to us and cares deeply about our lives. We also see how the chasm between God and us is graciously filled by God's revelation, which is more accurate and true than our human speculation (e.g., religion and philosophy). While the first step (Revelation/Inspiration of the autographa) is the only one that is guaranteed to be perfect, the other steps are indeed accurate and therefore trustworthy. We must be increasingly careful as we move through the steps, however, because the opportunity for error increases at each step. Lastly, the third step of translation is incredibly important because that is what we depend on for the learning and living of our Christian faith. This point will now be explored more fully.

8. Why Are There Different Bible Translations?

In translating the Bible into English, including the Old Testament, four general categories of translation are most common: word-for-word translations, thought-for-thought translations, paraphrases, and corruptions. The same four options are also used in the translation of other ancient books into English.

Word-for-Word

Word-for-word translations (also known as literal translations) make a special effort to carefully interpret each word from the original Greek, Hebrew, and Aramaic into English. Word-for-word translations emphasize God, the divine author of Scripture, over the human reader of Scripture. The result is a striving for the precision of what the Bible says, much like one would expect in other important communications, such as legal documents, marriage vows, or contracts. Word-for-word translations are generally at high school reading level.

Word-for-word translations tend to be the best for studying because of their accuracy, though they sometimes lose the poetic nuances of the original languages. The best-known word-for-word translation is the King James Version (KJV). However, because of its use of archaic English, it is very difficult for some people to read. Probably the best word-for-word translations are the English Standard Version (ESV), which I preach from, the New American Standard Bible (NASB), and the New King James Version (NKJV). Noted theologian and ESV General Editor J. I. Packer reflected, "I find myself suspecting very strongly that my work on the translation of the ESV Bible was the most important thing that I have done for the Kingdom, and that the product of our labors is perhaps the biggest milestone in Bible translation in the past fifty years or more."[130]

The philosophy of word-for-word translation guided virtually every English Bible translation until the middle of the twentieth century. At that time, thought-for-thought translation became popular.

Thought-for-Thought

Thought-for-thought translations (also known as dynamic equivalence or functional equivalence translations) attempt to convey the full nuance of each passage by interpreting the Scripture's entire meaning and not just the individual words. Thought-for-thought translations may include words that were not included in the original text in an effort to give the same meaning that the reader of the original languages would have had.

The best and most widely read thought-for-thought English translation is the New International Version (NIV). Other thought-for-thought translations include Today's New International Version (TNIV), New Living Translation (NLT), Contemporary English Version (CEV), and the Good News Bible (GNB). The benefit of thought-for-thought translations in general, and the NIV—my favorite thought-for-thought

130. Michelle Bennett, "The ESV Bible Reaches Five-Year Milestone," Good News and Crossway, September 26, 2006, http://www.gnpcb.org/page/news.2006.09.26.

translation—in particular, is that they are easy to understand and make the Bible accessible to a wide number of people.

Going one step further than thought-for-thought translations are paraphrases, which combine both Scripture and interpretive commentary into the translation method.

Paraphrase

Paraphrased translations pay even less attention to specific word meanings than thought-for-thought translations in an attempt to capture the poetic or narrative essence of a passage. For this reason, many paraphrased translations do not even have verse divisions in them. Examples of paraphrased translations include The Message (TM), The Living Bible (TLB), and The Amplified Bible (AMP).

Corruption

Corruptions are "translations" of Scripture that clearly seek to undermine the very teaching of Scripture. These "translations" are very poor and should not be used as credible translations for study. These include the Jehovah's Witness translation called the New World Translation, which was written in large part to eliminate the deity of Jesus Christ. This is in no way a translation but rather a terrible corruption of Scripture.

While some translations are better than others, it is important to note that various translations have various strengths and weaknesses and that the student of Scripture benefits from enjoying multiple translations. Furthermore, rather than fighting over translations, Christians should praise God for every good English translation and trust God the Holy Spirit to use them to transform our lives.

It is beneficial to one's studies to take advantage of multiple good English translations of Scripture. However, I would encourage you to use the English Standard Version or another good word-for-word translation as your primary study tool while using other translations as secondary resources for your studies. On this point it is important to be both clear and emphatic. The student of Scripture is best served by enjoying multiple translations of God's Word. Personally, I use both the English Standard Version and the New International Version most frequently, in addition to many other translations.

9. How Can I Get the Most Out of the Old Testament?

The remaining practical question pertains to what you can do to get the most out of the Old Testament. Before answering that question, I want to tell you a story about a peculiar German metalworker, inventor, and business entrepreneur named Johannes Gutenberg (1398–1468), who invented the moveable type printing press. His invention made the mass production of books, like this one, possible for the first time in human history.

Consider this for a moment. My personal library at my home is perhaps four thousand books and growing by the day thanks to God's grace and the guy in the brown truck who shows up every twenty-four hours. If we were living in 1450, my personal library would perhaps be the size of the library for many towns. At that time all books were hand-copied and took years to write out, with a Bible taking upwards of twenty years to complete. Consequently, all of the books in Western Europe totaled roughly the same number in a modern public library. But by 1500, the number of books exploded into the millions because Gutenberg's press, adapted from the presses used in wine making, enabled rapid printing. By 1500 there were 151 print shops in

Venice alone. In Martin Luther's city of Wittenberg, one hundred thousand Bibles were being printed.

Legend has it that as a little boy, Gutenberg was carving his name onto wooden blocks on his father's work bench when an "h" fell into a bucket of purple dye. Apparently Gutenberg took the block out of the dye bucket and set it on a piece of paper to dry, causing a stamp imprint that some forty years later would inspire him to create a metal press to print books in similar fashion.

Among the first things Gutenberg published were the now-famous Gutenberg Bibles in 1455. The two-volume Bibles had 1,282 pages and cost roughly the equivalent of three years' wages for a common worker. He printed two hundred copies on an expensive imported paper and thirty copies on vellum, which required the slaughter of ten thousand calves for their hides. To finance his start-up costs, Gutenberg borrowed a considerable amount of money. Shortly after his invention proved successful, his lender called in his debt, bankrupting Gutenberg and causing his printing presses to be seized. Tragically, Gutenberg never profited from his invention and died in poverty living off of a pension that was gifted to him by the Catholic Church.

Gutenberg's invention is among the most important in the history of the world. It sparked the information revolution, which led to the scientific revolution, the Renaissance, and the Protestant Reformation. At the end of 1999, A&E Biography named Gutenberg the most influential person of the millennium. Every time we pick up a printed document, especially a Bible, we honor his labor.

Therefore, the first step to getting the most out of the Old Testament is to recognize that it took roughly fifteen hundred years to be written, was hand-copied into manuscripts by scribes who devoted their life to that work, was translated by scholars who have devoted their lives to the biblical languages, and is published in mass market forms that have only been possible in the last half a millennium. In addition, many people died so that you could hold in your hand a copy of the Bible and read the Old

Testament for yourself. My fear is that in an age when the Bible is so readily and cheaply available, and in so many translations and forms, many people will overlook the incredible gift we have been given to be able to simply pick up the Bible and read it.

The second step to getting the most out of the Old Testament is to purchase a good Bible. While purchasing a study Bible can be quite expensive, it is imperative that all serious students of the Bible invest some money purchasing at least one nice Bible with some helps (footnotes, cross-references, etc.) and room for their own notes. When buying a Bible, the general rule is that the more money you spend, the better the quality of paper, binding, and leather you will receive. Because your primary Bible will be filled with notes and become so familiar to you, it is wise to invest in a good Bible that will last. If you cannot afford a good Bible, then perhaps asking your friends and family to chip in for a birthday or holiday such as Christmas to buy you one would be an option.

The third step to getting the most out of the Old Testament is knowing that Jesus actually prayed for you to do so. In John 17:17 Jesus prayed for us saying, "Sanctify them in the truth; your word is truth." Therefore, to increasingly grow to be more and more like Jesus, we must have regular time in God's Word. Practically, this means that when we read the Old Testament and in it meet Jesus, his prayer for us is being answered.

The fourth step is to practice the various spiritual disciplines that relate to Bible study. The Old Testament itself tells us to study, obey, and then teach the Scriptures.[131] It also models for us how to pray as we read Scripture, humbly asking God to teach us.[132] It promises to make us wiser.[133] The Old Testament also tells us that it is to be memorized.[134] To help you, you may want to listen to God's Word through an audio recording as you exercise, do chores, or commute to work, because faith, we are told

131. Ezra 7:10.
132. Ps. 119:73.
133. Prov. 9:9; 10:14; 23:12.
134. Ps. 119:11; Prov. 22:17–19.

in the New Testament, comes through hearing God's Word. Furthermore, because Jesus humbly entered into history as a human being, he had to grow and learn just like we do.[135] Subsequently, when we see Jesus frequently quoting the Old Testament from memory throughout his life, we must infer that he spent considerable amounts of time hearing, reading, studying, praying, memorizing, and obeying the Old Testament. We should gladly follow in his example.

The fifth step to getting the most out of the Old Testament is to repent of sin. As you read, God the Holy Spirit will convict you of sin in your life, including sins of commission where you are doing wrong, sins of omission where you are failing to do right, and sins of thought, word, deed, and motive. When you are convicted, your propensity will be to suppress the truth and continue on in sin.[136] But Jesus asks that we not harden our heart when he speaks to us, but rather humbly receive his words and respond in repentance. In repentance we are agreeing with God, thanking Jesus for dying to remove our sin, and trusting Jesus for the empowering grace of the Holy Spirit to enable us to live lives of obedience in conformity with Scripture and his example.

The sixth step to getting the most out of the Old Testament is being in the community of a local church with fellow Christians. Most of the Old Testament was written to communities of God's people and not just individuals. Although you do need a personal relationship with Jesus, you are also part of God's family, the church, which means that personal relationships with Jesus' people are also vital. By being actively involved in a church that is Bible-based and Jesus-centered, you will be able to serve others and be served, learn Scripture, and grow as a worshiper of Jesus in all of your life.

135. Luke 2:52.
136. Rom. 1:18.

2

How to Read the Old Testament

Having answered the most common questions about the Old Testament, I now hope to give you a brief overview of the various kinds of literature found therein, as well as a brief explanation of each Old Testament book.

The Pentateuch (Genesis, Exodus, Leviticus, Numbers, Deuteronomy)

The Pentateuch, meaning "one book in five parts," was written by Moses roughly fourteen hundred years before the birth of Jesus Christ. The Bible clearly states that Moses is the author of the Pentateuch: "When Moses had finished writing the words of this law in a book to the very end, Moses commanded the Levites who carried the ark of the covenant of the LORD, 'Take this Book of the Law and put it by the side of the ark of the covenant of the LORD your God. . . .'"[1] In this insightful section at the end of the Pentateuch, not only do we learn that Moses wrote the first five books of the Old Testament, but that these books were compiled as a single book and immediately recognized as God-given, perfect, and Scripture-worthy, to be placed alongside the very presence of God in the ark of the covenant. On other occasions the Bible also refers to the Pentateuch as a single book.[2]

Sadly, in the past few hundred years, critics have sought to convince people that Moses did not write the Pentateuch. However, Jesus taught that Moses did in fact

1. Deut. 31:24–26.
2. 2 Chron. 25:4; 35:12; Ezra 6:18; Neh. 13:1; Mark 12:26.

write the Pentateuch.[3] Jesus also repeatedly attributed sections of the Pentateuch to Mosaic authorship, including Exodus,[4] Leviticus,[5] and Deuteronomy.[6]

In addition to undermining confidence in the Mosaic authorship of the Pentateuch, critics have also sought to deny some of its most miraculous accounts. Nevertheless, Jesus clearly believed in and taught that even the most controversial portions of the Pentateuch are factual, such as Adam and Eve,[7] Cain and the murder of Abel,[8] Noah and the flood,[9] Abraham,[10] Sodom and Gomorrah,[11] Lot,[12] Isaac and Jacob,[13] the manna,[14] and healing by the wilderness serpent.[15]

In summary, the Pentateuch is one book in five parts all penned by Moses with God's inspiration as taught by Jesus Christ. Having established this fact we will now briefly examine each of the five books.

Genesis, the book of beginnings, is the first book of the Pentateuch and focuses on the life of Abraham and the patriarchs Isaac, Jacob, Joseph, and Judah, who were Abraham's descendants. Genesis covers roughly two thousand years and accounts for about 25 percent of the content of the Pentateuch. The remaining four books of the

3. John 5:46; 7:19.
4. Mark 7:10, cf. Ex. 20:12; Mark 12:26, cf. Ex. 3:6; Luke 20:37, cf. Ex. 3:6.
5. Matt. 8:4, cf. Leviticus 13–14; Mark 1:44, cf. Lev. 14:3; Luke 5:14, cf. Lev. 13:8, 14:4.
6. Matt. 19:8, cf. Deut. 24:1–4; Mark 7:10, cf. Deut. 5:16; Mark 10:4, cf. Deut. 24:1.
7. Matt. 19:4–5; Mark 10:6–8.
8. Matt. 23:35; Luke 11:51.
9. Matt. 24:37–39; Luke 17:26–27.
10. John 8:56.
11. Matt. 10:15; 11:23–24; Luke 10:12; 17:29.
12. Luke 17:28–32.
13. Matt. 8:11; Luke 13:28.
14. John 6:31, 49, 58.
15. John 3:14.

Pentateuch, Exodus through Deuteronomy, focus on the life of Moses and account for about 75 percent of the content of the Pentateuch. The men are an interesting juxtaposition: Abraham did not have the law but obeyed it by faith, while Moses did have the law but was punished for not obeying it.

Exodus is the sequel to Genesis. In Genesis, God promised that through Abraham he would create a people who would live in a land and be blessed after four hundred years in slavery.[16] The Exodus narrative opens in the midst of the Hebrew people's slavery under a tyrannical Pharaoh of Egypt.[17] In a moment of ignorance and arrogance, Pharaoh asked the fateful question, "Who is the Lord?"[18] It appears that God took this challenge seriously, and the entire Exodus story is his answer. Therefore, the primary theme of Exodus does not revolve around Moses or the Exodus event, but rather the revelation of God, that he might be known, feared, and worshiped by Egypt and Israel alike. Geographically, the Exodus story is easily divided into two primary scenes. The first scene is the Hebrews' stay in Egypt,[19] and the second scene is their journey in the wilderness.[20]

Leviticus derives its name from the tribe of Levi and is a litany of divine laws calling God's people to holiness that will grant them access to him. Subsequently, the word "holiness" dominates the book, along with the concept of access to God. Laws for sacrifices and offerings, priestly duties, dietary restrictions, purity, feasts, and the like

16. Gen. 15:13–14.
17. Ex. 1:1–15:21.
18. Ex. 5:2.
19. Ex. 1:1–15:21.
20. Ex. 15:22–40:38.

are prevalent in the book, which finds its explanation and fulfillment in the New Testament book of Hebrews.

Numbers takes the reader through the forty years of wilderness wanderings by the people of God. The book painfully demonstrates how sin prevents blessing. The sin of an entire generation caused it to forfeit its blessing of inheriting the Promised Land and to instead wander in the wilderness for forty years on a journey that should have taken only two weeks. After that generation died, the next generation was raised up to inherit the Promised Land of God.[21] Numbers shows that Israel was God's army raised up to take the Promised Land as an act of God's judgment on the godless Canaanites and proof of God's faithfulness to fulfill his promise to Abraham,[22] even in spite of sin.

Deuteronomy concludes the five books of the Pentateuch. The book is comprised mainly of sermons preached by Moses at the end of his life on the obligations of the new generation of God's people in their covenant with God. The book ends with the death and burial of Moses, which then sets the stage for the next book, Joshua, and the final arrival of God's people into their promised land.

The Pentateuch is composed of three literary styles: narrative, poetry, and law. The laws (numbering 611 or 613 depending upon how you count them) account for 68.5 percent of the entire Pentateuch. Jesus taught that these laws were written by Moses.[23] It is the function of these laws in the Christian life that has been a source of great theological debate. The proper use of the law is incredibly important, as 1 Timothy

21. Heb. 3:16–19.
22. Gen. 12:1–3.
23. John 7:19.

1:8 says: "we know that the law is good, *if* one uses it lawfully. . . ." The New Testament is clear that that law exists to show us our sin,[24] because sin is the breaking of the law.[25] However, the law cannot save someone because everyone but Jesus is a law-breaking sinner.[26] Jesus alone perfectly fulfilled the law.[27] When he died, Jesus, who was without sin, was punished in the place of his people as a substitute for their sins and took their sins and gave them his righteous and perfect obedience to the law.[28]

Consequently, salvation is given by faith in Jesus and grace from Jesus alone.[29] Then, by the grace of Jesus and power of the Holy Spirit, a Christian can begin to fulfill the demands of the law.[30] The primary means by which we fulfill the law is love.[31] In the end, the objective of the law is less about what we do and more about who we love. That is why when asked about the law, Jesus taught that the whole law was about us loving God and loving other people.[32]

In summary, Jesus is the God of the Pentateuch, its central theme, and who we are to love. Jesus taught this when he said, "If you believed Moses, you would believe me; for he wrote of me."[33] If we fail to connect the Pentateuch with Jesus, we stand with the teachers of the law in Jesus' day whom he rebuked for studying the Old Testament but failing to love him.[34] Conversely, if we faithfully connect the Pentateuch

24. Gal. 3:19–25.
25. 1 John 3:4.
26. Rom. 3:19–23.
27. Matt. 5:17–18.
28. 2 Cor. 5:21.
29. Eph. 2:8–9.
30. Rom. 8:3–7.
31. Rom. 13:10.
32. Matt. 22:37–39.
33. John 5:46.
34. John 5:39–47.

to Jesus, we will be following in the example he gave us after his resurrection when he taught how Moses revealed him.[35] The Pentateuch points to Jesus because he is the promised seed of Abraham,[36] he fulfills the law of Moses,[37] and he saves a multitude like Joseph.[38]

History (Joshua, Judges, Ruth, 1 Samuel, 2 Samuel, 1 Kings, 2 Kings, 1 Chronicles, 2 Chronicles, Ezra, Nehemiah, Esther)

The historical books were written over a period of roughly a millennium from Joshua (written around 1400 BC) to Esther (written around 450 BC). Through these books we see how God worked faithfully in the lives of his people. They are an encouragement for us to continually live by faith in God.

Joshua picks up where the Pentateuch ends. Joshua succeeds Moses as the leader of God's people and takes the new generation into the Promised Land.

Judges records the next painful season when God's people responded to his provision of their land by sinning against him so greatly that even the judges whom God appointed to oversee righteousness were tainted by the evil of the thankless people.

Ruth records God's providential hand over a widowed Moabite woman whose faith in God and extraordinary character caused Boaz to fall in love with her and redeem her life so that Jesus the Redeemer could be born through them.

35. Luke 24:25–47.
36. Acts 3:25–26; Rom. 1:2; Gal. 3:16.
37. Matt. 5:17.
38. Gen. 50:20.

1 Samuel continues to record the decline of Israel, including the capture of the sacred ark of God by the evil Philistines. God permitted this to occur as punishment of his people. He then established a monarchy to rule in his place, beginning with Saul.

2 Samuel records the death of Saul and the rise of David as king. David rules from the capital of Jerusalem and expresses a desire to build God's temple.

1 Kings records the rise of David's son, Solomon, who ruled during a season of unprecedented wealth and peace that included the construction of the temple. Solomon responded by falling into gross sin and idolatry, which led to the division of the kingdom into the two parts of Judah and Israel after his death. Judah and Israel both continued in unfaithfulness.

2 Kings opens with Elijah being taken up into heaven and Elisha succeeding him in prophetic ministry. It then recounts a series of mainly sinful kings who ruled in Judah and Israel until the godly King Josiah led a revival. That revival ended after his death when evil kings once again ruled and Babylon destroyed Jerusalem and the temple.

1 and 2 Chronicles were originally one book in the Hebrew Bible. The first book records the lack of blessing among God's people because of their many sins (e.g., ignored the Sabbath, did not rebuild the temple, married pagans, oppressed the poor, did not tithe). The second book compels them to faithfulness through a history lesson that includes David, Solomon, and godly kings.

Ezra and Nehemiah were one book in the Hebrew Bible. They record the Jews' return to Judah after Babylonian captivity (which was punishment for sin), the rebuilding of Jerusalem's walls, and the institution of religious reforms.

Esther is the amazing story of how God's people were spared from extermination by the providential marriage of a young Jewish orphan to the king of Persia, thereby preserving the family line through which Jesus would be born.

Wisdom (Job, Psalms, Proverbs, Ecclesiastes, Song of Songs)

The wisdom literature is intensely practical, experiential, reflective, personal, and honest. It predates the Greeks (e.g., Epimenides, Socrates, Plato, Aristotle) as the first and greatest philosophy, probing deep existential issues such as the meaning of life (Ecclesiastes), the problem of suffering (Job), the nature of wisdom (Proverbs), love and sexual pleasure (Song of Songs), and worship (Psalms).

Next to story, poetry is the most common type of literature in the Bible and is quite common throughout the wisdom literature. Some wisdom literature books are entirely poetic, such as Psalms, Song of Songs, and Proverbs. Other wisdom literature books are almost entirely poetic, such as Job and Ecclesiastes. Most of the wisdom literature was written by David (Psalms) and his son Solomon (Proverbs, Ecclesiastes, Song of Songs). Both men are curiously well known for both their great wisdom and their foolish sexual sin.

The wisdom literature directly relates to Jesus because he alone is admittedly wiser than Solomon.[39] In fact, there can be no pursuit of wisdom apart from Jesus because he is our Wisdom.[40]

Job may be the first book of the Bible that was written (perhaps 1800–1500 BC), and it addresses the great philosophical questions surrounding the suffering of the righteous.

39. Matt. 12:42.
40. 1 Cor. 1:30; Col. 2:3.

Psalms is a collection of 150 songs compiled over a lengthy period of Old Testament history by various authors, including David, whom God inspired to pen the worship songs of God's people. These include hymns of praise, laments of grief, declarations of thanksgiving, and songs of confidence in God, remembrance of God, and living by wisdom in God, who is often referred to as the King.

Proverbs includes a vast number of truisms about practical life issues—such as friendship, work, wealth, marriage, and sex—and how we can live wisely if we obey God out of redeemed hearts that fear him.

Ecclesiastes answers the great philosophical question about the meaning of life and reveals that good things and the ability to enjoy them are two different things, like a box of chocolates and a mouth. Therefore, unless we obey God, life will be continually frustrating no matter how much power, wisdom, food, drink, sex, and riches we acquire.

The Song of Songs is a great series of poetic love songs exchanged between Solomon and his bride. Without descending into crudeness, the Song of Songs frankly discusses everything from oral sex to a wife who enjoys stripping for her husband and making love outdoors.

Prophets and Prophecy

Roughly 25 percent of the Bible was prophetic at the time it was written, meaning that it foretold future events. Therefore, it is very important to understand both prophets and prophecy if we want to understand a large portion of the Old Testament. I have chosen to spend considerable time explaining both prophets and prophecy for two reasons. First, there is much confusion among Christians, particularly new Christians, regarding what constitutes true and false prophets and prophecy. Second, it is not uncommon for the bookstores in our spiritual age to be filled with non-biblical authors who claim to be acting in a prophetic manner by revealing the future, speaking on behalf of God, and writing sacred texts. With this brief explanation of prophets and prophecy, I hope to help you both understand the Bible and distinguish it from imposters. Much of the information in this section is taken from the book *Toward Rediscovering the Old Testament*, one of many outstanding books written by the great Old Testament scholar, Walter Kaiser.[41]

In Israel, it was the ministry of the prophets to intercede for God before the people, to offer his Word as a light to expose the darkness of their sins, and to point them to the promises of the coming Messiah, Jesus. Sadly, the prophets have often been misrepresented as mere futuristic prognosticators who could foretell the future like some cheap circus sideshow fortune teller. Indeed, the prophets often did foretell the future, though this was not the majority of their ministry. Instead, the bulk of their ministry was spent proclaiming God's Word, by the power of God's Spirit, from the deep pain of God's heart over sin. God used the shouts of the prophets to awaken his slumbering people and provoke their imaginations to the life that he intended for them but that they had frequently neglected in favor of sin.

The prophetic calling was the combination of two ministries. First, the prophets received specific revelation directly from God. Second, they spoke or wrote that revealed Word to God's people. The prophets were painfully aware of the weightiness of their call because they consciously knew that they were the very mouth of Almighty

41. Walter C. Kaiser, *Toward Rediscovering the Old Testament* (Grand Rapids, MI: Zondervan, 1991).

God and spoke for him. This is clearly seen with Moses,[42] Isaiah,[43] Jeremiah,[44] Amos,[45] and Zechariah.[46]

The prophets preached because they were compelled to. God burned his Word so deeply into their hearts and minds that they could do nothing but speak. As Amos said, "The lion has roared; who will not fear? The Lord GOD has spoken; who can but prophesy?"[47] Perhaps Jeremiah articulated this compulsion best, saying, "If I say, 'I will not mention him, or speak any more in his name,' there is in my heart as it were a burning fire shut up in my bones, and I am weary with holding it in, and I cannot."[48]

The prophets preached the very words of God. According to the Old Testament scholar Gerhard von Rad, the phrase "the word of Yahweh" appears 241 times in the Old Testament, 221 of which are in relation to a prophet.[49]

Unlike priests who were selected by their family origins,[50] prophets had only the call of God to legitimize their ministry. Their call was not predicated on prior ministry testing or ability.[51] A number of basic elements describe the prophetic call. They did not seek their office.[52] They did not always like the message they were called to speak.[53]

42. Ex. 4:16; 7:1–2.
43. Isa. 1:20.
44. Jer. 1:7.
45. Amos 3:8; 7:16.
46. Zech. 7:12.
47. Amos 3:8.
48. Jer. 20:9.
49. Gerhard von Rad, *The Message of the Prophets* (New York: Harper & Row, 1965), 66.
50. Ex. 28:1; Leviticus 21–22.
51. Amos 7:14.
52. Amos 7:14–15.
53. Jonah 1–4.

They did not always understand their own message.[54] They often endured extreme hardship, such as Hosea marrying a prostitute to illustrate a point.[55] They often struggled deeply with their call, like Jeremiah who at times viewed his call as an unfair hardship.[56] They were also persecuted, as when Jeremiah's neighbors spoke evil about him and plotted to kill him[57] and when Daniel was thrown into a lions' den.[58] The prophetic call also included supernatural occurrences, such as the calling of their name,[59] God speaking,[60] the touch of God,[61] being seized by God,[62] and the Spirit of God coming upon them.[63]

Jesus,[64] Paul,[65] and John[66] all promised that false prophets would come just as they had in the days of the Old Testament. The presence of false prophets in every age suggests that the people of God must always distinguish the true from the false prophets. This task is difficult since the false prophets claim many of the same qualifications as the true prophets. Like true prophets, false prophets claim to speak for God.[67] Also, Satan can perform false miracles,[68] like when Pharaoh's sorcerers and

54. Dan. 7:15–16; 12:8; 1 Pet. 1:10–11.
55. Hosea 1–3.
56. Jer. 20:7–18.
57. Jer. 11:18–19; 18:18.
58. Daniel 6.
59. 1 Sam. 3:4.
60. Isa. 5:9; 22:14; Ezek. 9:1, 5.
61. 1 Kings 18:46; Ezek. 8:1.
62. Isa. 8:11.
63. Num. 24:2; 2 Kings 3:15.
64. Matt. 7:15; 24:11, 24.
65. Acts 20:29–31.
66. 1 John 4:1.
67. 1 Kings 22.
68. Deut. 13:1–3; 2 Thess. 2:9; Rev. 13:13–15.

magicians turned their staffs into snakes like Aaron had.[69] Therefore, simply because a prophet can perform miracles does not necessarily prove that he acts by the power of God.

While no one single test for the authentication of a prophet is appropriate, a few criteria help distinguish between true and false prophets. A true prophet had outstanding moral character,[70] while false prophets did not.[71] The prophecy of a true prophet came true every time, while false prophets were hit and miss.[72] False prophets were for hire and preached what they were paid to preach,[73] such as always prophesying peace and prosperity.[74] The message of a false prophet conflicted with God's prior revelation, led to the worship of false gods, and was punishable by death.[75] For further insights on the differences between true and false prophets, a careful reading of Deuteronomy 18:14–22 and Jeremiah 23:9–40 is very helpful.

Today, Christians can discern between true and false prophets by the inward testimony of the Holy Spirit.[76] Since both a believing hearer and a true prophet are filled with the Spirit, it is sensible to assume that the Spirit in a Christian would confirm that the message was true.

Now that we have established a proper understanding of prophets and prophecy, we will continue by examining the prophetic books of the Old Testament. We will begin with the major prophets, whose works are generally older and longer than those of the minor prophets.

69. Ex. 7:8–13.
70. Ezek. 13:10–16.
71. Isa. 28:7.
72. Deuteronomy 18; 1 Kings 22; Jeremiah 28.
73. Mic. 3:11.
74. Jer. 6:13–14; 8:10–11.
75. Deuteronomy 13.
76. Deut. 18:14–22; John 7:17.

Major Prophets (Isaiah, Jeremiah, Lamentations, Ezekiel, Daniel)

Isaiah is widely considered the prince of the Old Testament prophets. His ministry lasted roughly sixty years and is alluded to some four hundred times in the New Testament. The lengthy book bearing his name can be divided into two sections: humiliating punishment for sin (Isaiah 1–39) and redeeming salvation for individuals, communities, and nations through Jesus the Suffering Servant (Isaiah 40–66).

Because so many college students routinely ask if Isaiah actually wrote the book of Isaiah, I will briefly explain this issue. Some "scholars" have postulated that two authors wrote Isaiah and they divide the book into two works of chapters 1–39 and chapters 40–66. Others have postulated that there were three authors, and they divide the book into three works of chapters 1–39, 40–55, and 56–66. However, as the following chart clearly shows, the Gospels quote directly from Isaiah on eight occasions and attribute those writings to Isaiah himself. These quotes include two references from Jesus himself stating that Isaiah wrote Isaiah (Matt. 13:14–15 and 15:7–9). Half of the eight quotes

Chart 2.1 *The Gospels and Isaiah*

Gospel Teaching	Cross-Reference in Isaiah
Matthew 3:3	Isaiah 40:3
Matthew 4:14–15	Isaiah 9:1–2
Matthew 8:17	Isaiah 53:4
Matthew 12:17–21	Isaiah 42:1–4
Matthew 13:14–15	Isaiah 6:9–10
Matthew 15:7–9	Isaiah 29:13
John 12:38	Isaiah 53:1
John 12:39–41	Isaiah 6:10

are taken from Isaiah 1–39 and half are taken from Isaiah 40–66. Concerning chapters 56–66, Jesus actually reads from Isaiah 61:1–2 in Luke 4:17–19, and Luke attributes that section of Scripture to the authorship of Isaiah. Chart 2.1 shows how often the Gospels attribute a section of Isaiah to the authorship of Isaiah.

Therefore, if Isaiah did not pen Isaiah, then Jesus is a bad Bible teacher and not up to the standards of the grad student teaching the "Bible as Literature" class to freshmen at the local community college.

Jeremiah is the weeping prophet whose heart is broken by the sin of his day. His book is not arranged chronologically nor topically and is, therefore, very difficult to outline, but generally falls into three groupings: the charges of sin against God's people (Jer. 1:1–25:13), consolation from the new covenant (Jeremiah 30–31), and prophecies against the nations (Jeremiah 46–51). Biographical interludes occur in chapters 26–29 and chapters 32–45.

Lamentations is also written by Jeremiah and is a collection of some of the most painfully honest poetry ever penned by a man who loved God, hated sin, and was emotionally devastated to stand with God in looking upon the evil among God's people in his day.

Ezekiel was both a priest and a prophet who prophesied for some twenty years during a time of captivity in Babylon. He wrote to proclaim that God's people no longer experienced God's glory because of sin (chapters 1–24), to announce God's judgment on nations surrounding Judah in preparation for the return of God's glory (chapters 25–32), and to describe the return of God's glory and the restoration of Israel (chapters 33–48).

Daniel prophesied for some sixty-nine years (the longest of any prophet) during Babylonian captivity. He was a contemporary of both Ezekiel and Jeremiah. The book records his interpretation of dreams (chapters 1–6) and visions from God about Jesus coming as the King to establish his kingdom and crush all godless kingdoms (chapters 7–12).

Minor Prophets (Hosea, Joel, Amos, Obadiah, Jonah, Micah, Nahum, Habakkuk, Zephaniah, Haggai, Zechariah, Malachi)

Hosea is nearly all poetry and records the shocking event of God's prophet Hosea marrying the prostitute Gomer. Their relationship illustrates Israel's unfaithfulness to God and God's continued devotion to his people—a bride that he faithfully loves.

Joel records the plague of locusts that God sent as punishment for sin in Joel's day,[77] as well as future events related to the "day of the Lord" when God will bring history to an end by punishing sin and ushering in his kingdom.[78]

Amos is a call to repentance among God's people who had fallen into a heartless and empty ritualism and who had become financially rich but spiritually poor. It ends, though, with a note of hope for the day when Jesus rules from David's throne.

Obadiah is one chapter of poetic prophecy detailing God's displeasure and subsequent judgment upon the nation of Edom for warring against God's people.

77. Joel 1:1–2:27.
78. Joel 2:18–3:21.

Jonah is the account of the greatest mass conversion in the Bible in the godless Assyrian capital of Nineveh through the preaching of the racist and rebellious prophet Jonah, who eventually came to repentance before writing the book.

Micah preached to both the kingdoms of Israel and Judah during a time of great sin and apathy, and his book breaks into three sermons (Mic. 1:2; 3:1; 6:1), each beginning with a call to "hear," that threaten judgment to sinners and offer mercy to those who repent.

Nahum is a short promise of judgment against the Assyrian capital of Nineveh for repeatedly persecuting and harming God's people without remorse.

Habakkuk records a series of conversations between a godly man and the Lord during a dark time of national sin. It focuses on the need to trust God in faith,[79] which becomes a great theme quoted in the New Testament.[80]

Zephaniah is a short promise of universal judgment for sin on the "day of the Lord" to warn those who falsely believed that God would not act to redeem his people and judge unrepentant sinners.

Haggai is a series of four sermons (Hag. 1:1; 2:1; 2:10; 2:20) commanding the few people who returned to Judah after Babylonian captivity to rebuild the temple in preparation for Jesus' coming.

79. Hab. 2:4.
80. Rom. 1:17; Gal. 3:11; Heb. 10:38.

Zechariah began preaching as a young man.[81] His book records a series of visions intended to motivate the rebuilding of the temple and repentant hearts among the Jews.[82] Zechariah offers a glimpse into the end of time and the coming of the King Jesus who would destroy evil,[83] which explains why he is referenced some thirty-one times in the New Testament book of Revelation.

Malachi is the final Old Testament book. It closes with the promise that John the Baptizer would come to prepare the way for Jesus. Malachi also prophecies that the expected Messiah would go to the temple. Jesus fulfilled this prophecy a matter of years before the temple was destroyed, thereby proving that he alone could be the promised Messiah.[84]

In conclusion, it is my sincere hope that this booklet has helped introduce you to the Old Testament and has inspired you to read it for yourself. As you do, I pray God will reveal himself to you and that you will love Jesus and your neighbors because that is ultimately why God inspired it to be written.

81. Zech. 2:4.
82. Zechariah 1–8.
83. Zechariah 9–14.
84. Mal. 3:1, cf. Matt. 3:1–17, 17:9–13, Luke 1:8–17.

Appendix 1

Building a Theological Library

In writing a letter to his friend Timothy who was coming to visit him, Paul urged Timothy to bring both his Bible and his books. Indeed, while the Bible is the most important collection of books, other books—particularly reference books—are also incredibly helpful in your study of the books of the Bible. As a new Christian in college I began by simply reading through the Bible in an effort to get a macro view of its content. Then, I chose one book of the Bible that most interested me and devoted myself to studying it exclusively until I felt that I had a good understanding of that book. After studying a particular book of the Bible for enough months to familiarize myself, I then chose another book and repeated the process. I have been doing this simple routine ever since, and out of it has come my Bible teaching ministry, pulpit, and Mars Hill Church.

I would encourage you to undertake a similar process with a lifelong goal of taking an average of six months to invest in each book of the Bible. Some books will take you longer to study, while others will require only a matter of weeks because of their brevity. By devoting an average of six months to each book, you will study the entire Bible in roughly thirty-three years.

To build a good basic theological library you will need to spend some money. You may find that friends and family are helpful in this process, especially if you ask for specific books for your birthday and other holidays. Thankfully, we live in a time when there is an abundance of good Bible reference material. But there is also a lot of junk. After working at a theological bookstore and also building a personal library of roughly four thousand volumes, I hope the following recommendations will help you invest your money wisely.

To begin, you should buy the books in the following order that they appear and purchase one from each section. At the end of this list I have also included some Web sites and other ideas that will help save you money as you build your library. There are also some books you will want to purchase that review the very best reference material available. By consulting these books you will save yourself a great deal of time and money. John Glynn's *Commentary and Reference Survey* (Grand Rapids, MI: Kregel, 2007) reviews the best books in the major areas of theology and the best commentaries on every book of the Bible. If you hope to do advanced study or build a larger library, this resource is indispensable. Tremper Longman III also has written the *Old Testament Commentary Survey* (Grand Rapids, MI: Baker, 2007), and my friend D. A. Carson has written the *New Testament Commentary Survey* (Grand Rapids, MI: Baker, 2007). I commend each of these three books before you begin building your theological library.

Buying a Good Bible

To get started, you need to have a good Bible that you can keep for years and in which you can take notes. You will also want to get a few other translations of the Bible in inexpensive formats (e.g., used or paperback copies) to help compare translations. You can also purchase a parallel Bible that puts multiple translations side by side in one Bible. The following recommendations should help you get a good Bible:

1. Get your primary Bible in the English Standard Version (ESV) translation because it is an accurate translation that is also very readable.

2. Get good leather, not a bonded type of leather or leather that's been dyed in some strange color like pink or blue because cows those colors live near nuclear plants.
3. Get a well-bound Bible so that it does not fall apart as you use it.
4. Get a good study Bible that you like. There are a number of study Bibles, and the best ones have a great deal of helpful information.
5. You get what you pay for, so plan on spending some money on a good Bible.

Reading through the Entire Bible

It is not uncommon for people who are new to the Bible to simply pick it up and begin reading forward from Genesis, like any other book. But it is also not uncommon for them to throw their hands in the air in Leviticus because they have become completely lost somewhere between the regulations on cleaning the mildew from your home for God and the command for defiled men to bathe themselves in a river. While it is true that all Scripture is God-breathed and profitable, it is also true that some parts are tough to navigate without a map. The following books will help you read through the entire Bible and get a macro view of its content. The first is very simple, and the second is a bit more informative.

- *What the Bible is All About*, by Henrietta C. Mears (Ventura, CA: Regal, 2007), is a great beginning place for people who are relatively unfamiliar with their Bible. It provides a simple introduction to each book and lists the essential chapters of that book of the Bible that should be read.
- *How to Read the Bible Book by Book*, by Gordon D. Fee and Douglas Stuart (Grand Rapids, MI: Zondervan, 2002), also takes you through each book of the Bible and does so in a more thorough fashion than Mears's book.

How to Study the Bible

After you have read your Bible enough to have a general understanding of its primary themes, you then need to learn how to dig deeper and study books, chapters, and verses of your Bible. Fortunately, there are a wide number of excellent books that teach you how to study your Bible.

- *Getting the Message*, by Daniel M. Doriani (Phillipsburg, NJ: P&R, 1996), teaches you how to study different types of books in the Bible and includes practical assignments.
- *Grasping God's Word*, by J. Scott Duvall and John Daniel Hays (Grand Rapids, MI: Zondervan, 2005), is an excellent tool for teaching you how to study the Bible.
- *Reading the Bible with Heart and Mind*, by Tremper Longman III (Colorado Springs, CO: NavPress, 1996), is a simple introduction on how to study the Bible.

Bible Dictionaries

These reference materials are full of maps, charts, pictures, cultural insights, and basic language helps (Hebrew, Aramaic, and Greek). They are designed to provide the student with specific information on a wide variety of biblical subjects. A good dictionary is an essential reference piece to have in your library and will be continually useful. There are a number of good Bible dictionaries that range from one volume to multiple volumes. The following are some of the best:

- *The New Bible Dictionary,* edited by I. Howard Marshall et al. (Downer's Grove, IL: InterVarsity Press, 1996), is a one-volume Bible dictionary.

- *The New Unger's Bible Dictionary*, by Merril Unger (Chicago, IL: Moody, 2006) is an update of the classic one-volume Bible dictionary.
- *Zondervan's Pictorial Encyclopedia of the Bible*, edited by Merrill Tenney (Grand Rapids, MI: Zondervan, 1975), is a full five volumes in length. If the cost of this reference piece deters you, it may be worthwhile to consider buying it in CD-ROM format, which is less expensive.

Concordances

A concordance is a collection of the most common words found in the Old and New Testaments. An exhaustive concordance will list each word found in Scripture and all of its occurrences. By using a numbering system, some concordances will identify the actual Hebrew or Greek word that has been translated into English. For instance, though there are three different Greek words used in the New Testament for "love" (each having its own nuance), our English texts translate them all the same way. A good concordance will show those distinctions. The concordance you choose will have to match up with the Bible version you study from (most major versions have concordances available). Make sure that you buy an exhaustive concordance to ensure that every word of your Bible is included and that it is in the translation of the Bible that you will be using primarily.

Topical Bible

A topical Bible will help you find all the verses in the Bible on particular subjects. The classic reference material in this category is *Nave's Topical Bible* by Orville J. Nave (Nashville: Thomas Nelson, 2003), which you will likely find at a used bookstore, as well as new.

Cross-Reference

One of the best ways to study the Bible is to let the Scriptures interpret the Scriptures. To do this you will enjoy *The Treasury of Scriptural Knowledge* (McLean, VA: MacDonald, 1982), which takes every verse of the Bible and cross-references it with all of the other verses in the Bible that relate to that verse. This classic reference work can be commonly found in used bookstores, as well as new.

Bible Atlas

As you read the Bible you will quickly see how often places are mentioned throughout it. A Bible atlas will help you see where those places are and how they relate to each other geographically. I recommend the following:

- *The Holman Bible Atlas* by Thomas C. Brisco (Nashville: Broadman & Holman, 1999).
- *Baker's Bible Atlas* by Charles F. Pfeiffer (Grand Rapids, MI: Baker, 2003).

New Testament Surveys

A New Testament survey provides an outline of each book in the New Testament, introducing the authors, books, and historical settings of each book. This reference is a great place to start when beginning to study a book of the Bible.

- *An Introduction to the New Testament* by D. A. Carson and Douglas J. Moo (Grand Rapids, MI: Zondervan, 2005).
- *A Survey of the New Testament* by Robert H. Gundry (Grand Rapids, MI: Zondervan, 2003).

- *New Testament Introduction* by Donald Guthrie (Downers Grove, IL: Inter-Varsity Press, 1990).
- *An Introduction to the New Testament* by David A. deSilva (Downers Grove, IL: InterVarsity Press, 2004).

Old Testament Surveys

Old Testament surveys provide an introduction to each book of the Old Testament, including information such as the date of their writing, authorship, historical context, main themes, and book outline. They also provide an overview of the theological debates surrounding the Old Testament and recommend further reading for Old Testament studies.

- *A Survey of the Old Testament* by Andrew E. Hill and John H. Walton (Grand Rapids, MI: Zondervan, 2000).
- *An Introduction to the Old Testament* by Tremper Longman III and Raymond D. Dillard (Grand Rapids, MI: Zondervan, 2006).
- *Old Testament Theology* by Paul R. House (Downers Grove, IL: InterVarsity Press, 1990).

Preaching and Teaching the Old Testament

For those who preach and teach the Bible, the following resources are quite helpful in learning how to connect the Old Testament to Jesus.

- *Preaching Christ from the Old Testament* by Sidney Greidanus (Grand Rapids, MI: Eerdmans, 1999).
- *Preaching Christ in All of Scripture* by Edmund P. Clowney (Wheaton, IL: Crossway, 2003).

- *Christ-Centered Preaching* by Bryan Chapell (Grand Rapids, MI: Baker, 2005).
- *Preaching the Whole Bible as Christian Scripture* by Graeme Goldsworthy (Grand Rapids, MI: Eerdmans, 2000).

Studies on the Old Testament

These Old Testament studies provide a theological overview and understanding of the Old Testament.

- *Toward Rediscovering the Old Testament* by Walter C. Kaiser (Grand Rapids, MI: Zondervan, 1991).
- *Gospel and Kingdom: A Christian Guide of the Old Testament* by Graeme Goldsworthy (San Francisco, CA: Harper, 1983).
- *He Gave Us Stories*, by Richard L. Pratt Jr. (Phillipsburg, NJ: P&R, 1993), is an introduction on how to connect the Old Testament narratives to Jesus.
- *The Pentateuch as Narrative*, by John H. Sailhamer (Grand Rapids, MI: Zondervan, 1995), is an introduction to and commentary on the first five books of the Old Testament.
- *The Shadow of Christ in the Law of Moses*, by Vern S. Poythress (Phillipsburg, NJ: P&R, 1995), shows how the laws of Moses point to Jesus.

Manners and Customs

These reference books provide a wealth of information about the customs and lifestyles of biblical times. They often function as Bible dictionaries or encyclopedias, yet may have more cultural information than those reference tools have.

- Alfred Edersheim is a well-respected classic author whose books *The Life and Times of Jesus the Messiah* (Peabody, MA: Hendrickson, 1993) and *Sketches of Jewish Social Life in the Time of Christ* (West Valley City, UT: The Editorium, 2006) are very helpful for understanding the culture in which the Bible was written. Because these are classic reference works, it is common to find them in used bookstores, as well as new.
- *The New Manners and Customs of Bible Times*, by Ralph Gower (Chicago, IL: Moody, 2005), is also a well-respected classic reference book.
- *Dictionary of Biblical Imagery*, edited by Leland Ryken, James C. Wilhoit, and Tremper Longman III (Downers Grove, IL: InterVarsity Press, 1998), is an invaluable resource for understanding the manners and customs of Bible times.
- *The IVP Bible Background Commentary: Old Testament*, by John H. Walton, Victor H. Matthews, and Mark Chavalas (Downers Grove, IL: InterVarsity Press, 2000), is a verse-by-verse explanation of various Old Testament cultural customs.
- *The IVP Bible Background Commentary: New Testament*, by Craig S. Keener (Downers Grove, IL: InterVarsity Press, 1994), is a verse-by-verse explanation of various New Testament cultural customs.

Commentaries

Commentaries go through a book of the Bible chapter by chapter and verse by verse in an effort to explain what is said. Commentaries are designed to help the student after proper study has been done and should never take the place of your own personal time in the Word. They should be used with caution and discretion because, unlike the Bible, they are not perfect. Some commentaries are very helpful, while others are so erroneous that they will do little more than confuse and frustrate you. However, good commentaries—like good Bible teachers—can prove to be extremely helpful for the student to gain cultural, grammatical, and historical insights into the text. It can also be helpful to see others' views that challenge us and cause us to think about our own conclusions. There are literally hundreds of individual commentaries on the books of the Bible, so trying to choose one is quite difficult. As a general rule, any single-volume commentary or multi-volume commentary series that has multiple authors who specialize in different books of the Bible will be the best use of your money. To help you navigate through the myriad of commentaries, I would again encourage you to consult John Glynn's *Commentary and Reference Survey* (Grand Rapids, MI: Kregel, 2007) and possibly Tremper Longman's *Old Testament Commentary Survey* (Grand Rapids, MI: Baker, 2007) and D. A. Carson's *New Testament Commentary Survey* (Grand Rapids, MI: Baker, 2007) before purchasing any single- or multiple-volume commentaries.

Bible Difficulties

Some portions of the Bible are often attacked for being inaccurate and/or contradictory to other parts of the Bible. Therefore, it is helpful to have a solid reference book that seeks to provide faithful answers to these tough texts. At least one of the following books is essential to include in your library.

- *When Critics Ask*, by Norman Geisler and Thomas Howe (Grand Rapids, MI: Baker, 1992), is arguably the best book on Bible difficulties.
- *Hard Sayings of the Bible*, by Walter C. Kaiser Jr. et al., (Downers Grove, IL: InterVarsity Press, 1996), is a very good reference book.
- *New International Encyclopedia of Bible Difficulties*, by Gleason L. Archer Jr. (Grand Rapids, MI: Zondervan, 2001), is also quite good.

Systematic Theology

Systematic theology is the process of taking the related concepts and verses from the Bible and collecting them together according to topic. Systematic theology is very important to your understanding of the Bible, and having at least one good systematic theology is vital to every library. There are a multitude of such texts, and as you grow in your studies you will likely add many of these to your library. The ones recommended below are a great start.

- *Systematic Theology*, by Wayne Grudem (Grand Rapids, MI: Zondervan, 1995), is a thorough work.
- *Christian Theology*, by Millard J. Erickson (Grand Rapids, MI: Baker, 1998), is a classic introduction to systematic theology.
- *Integrative Theology,* by Gordon R. Lewis and Bruce A. Demarest (Grand Rapids, MI: Zondervan, 1996), is a great look at theology from multiple disciplines.

The Canon and Manuscripts

- *The Canon of Scripture*, by F. F. Bruce (Downers Grove, IL: InterVarsity Press, 1988), is a thorough explanation of why some books are in the Bible and others are not.
- *The Indestructible Book*, by W. Kenneth Connolly (Grand Rapids, MI: Baker, 1996), is a fascinating historical look at how the Scriptures have been both opposed and adored over the ages.
- *The New Testament Documents: Are They Reliable?* by F. F. Bruce (Downers Grove, IL: InterVarsity Press, 1981), is a helpful study on the number and quality of New Testament manuscripts.

- *The Authority of the New Testament Scriptures*, by Herman Ridderbos (Grand Rapids, MI: Baker, 1963), is very helpful in understanding the trustworthiness of the New Testament manuscripts.
- *The Historical Reliability of the Gospels* by Craig L. Blomberg (Downers Grove, IL: InterVarsity Press, 2008).
- *The Text of the New Testament: Its Transmission, Corruption, and Restoration* by Bruce M. Metzger and Bart D. Ehrman (New York: Oxford University Press, 2005).

Bible Translations

- *Pastoral Reflections on Bible Translations* by Mark Driscoll at www.theresurgence.com.
- *The Indestructible Book* by W. Kenneth Connolly (Grand Rapids, MI: Baker, 1996).
- *The Word of God in English* by Leland Ryken (Wheaton, IL: Crossway, 2002).
- *Choosing a Bible* by Leland Ryken (Wheaton, IL: Crossway, 2005).
- *The Bible in Translation* by Bruce M. Metzger (Grand Rapids, MI: Baker, 2001).
- *How We Got the Bible* by John H. Sailhamer (Grand Rapids, MI: Zondervan, 1998).
- *A General Introduction to the Bible* by Norman Geisler and William E. Nix (Chicago, IL: Moody, 1986).

The Divine Inspiration of Scripture

- *God Has Spoken: Revelation and the Bible* by J. I. Packer (Grand Rapids, MI: Baker, 1994).

- *Inerrancy,* edited by Norman L. Geisler (Grand Rapids, MI: Zondervan, 1980), is a helpful collection of essays.
- *Christ and the Bible*, by John Wenham (Grand Rapids, MI: Baker, 1994), is a very helpful survey of how Jesus Christ viewed the Old Testament.

Biblical and Theological Jargon

As you begin to study theology you will discover that, like every discipline, it is filled with its own jargon and vocabulary that must be understood. The following books can help you reference tough words that are unfamiliar to you.

- *Zondervan Dictionary of Bible and Theology Words* by Matthew S. DeMoss and J. Edward Miller (Grand Rapids, MI: Zondervan, 2002).
- *The Compact Dictionary of Doctrinal Words*, by Terry L. Miethe (Bloomington, MN: Bethany, 1988), is succinct and to the point.

Software

There is a large and growing repository of excellent Bible software for everyone from the simple student to the most adept scholar. The prices and features vary greatly, and the software upgrades continually. You will also find that some Bible software companies offer inexpensive software packages that bundle together many of the reference materials that I recommended above. As a result, for those who are computer savvy, buying the right software is generally the most inexpensive and efficient way to build a theological library. The following Web sites will help get you started on researching good Bible software.

- www.logos.com
- www.biblesoft.com
- www.bibleworks.com

Web Sites with Free Bible Study Resources

There is a seemingly infinite number of free Web sites that help you study the Bible. The following are a few recommendations to get you started.

- www.bible.org. Click on the "Net Bible" section for access to many Bible study tools.
- bible.crosswalk.com. Multiple translations, concordances, an interlinear Bible, a parallel Bible, commentaries, dictionaries, encyclopedias, lexicons.
- www.biblegateway.com. Multiple translations and concordances, a topical Bible.
- www.bibleplaces.com. Maps and pictures of places in the Bible.
- www.carm.org. Has an enormous library of articles on a wide variety of Christian issues.
- www.ccel.org. Contains an enormous number of classic Christian books. The online study Bible is among the best ways to see what the best theologians in the church have said about a particular text of the Bible.
- www.christianitytoday.com/bible. Bibles, concordances, dictionaries, lexicons, commentaries, apologetics, etc.
- www.danielakin.com. A variety of resources for Bible study, including an extensive list for "Building a Theological Library."
- www.equip.org. Articles on cults, theology, and just about anything else.
- www.esv.org. The online collection of Bible study tools associated with the English Standard Version of the Bible.
- www.theresurgence.com. Hosted by the church I pastor, this has an enormous library of resources on theological issues in print, audio, and video format from some of today's top Bible teachers.

- www.studylight.org. Bible dictionaries, interlinear Bibles, parallel Bibles, commentaries, concordances, encyclopedias, lexicons.
- www.webbible.net. Translations and concordances, commentaries, parallel Bibles, Greek and Hebrew tools, a Bible chronology.
- www.zhubert.com. An amazing Web site built by one of the elders of our church that allows you to study the original languages of the Bible at no charge.

Appendix 2

Old Testament Reading Checklist

The following checklist is offered to help you track your personal reading of the Old Testament.

Genesis																			
1	2	3	4	5	6	7	8	9	10	11	12	13	14	15	16	17	18	19	20
21	22	23	24	25	26	27	28	29	30	31	32	33	34	35	36	37	38	39	40
41	42	43	44	45	46	47	48	49	50										

Exodus																			
1	2	3	4	5	6	7	8	9	10	11	12	13	14	15	16	17	18	19	20
21	22	23	24	25	26	27	28	29	30	31	32	33	34	35	36	37	38	39	40

Leviticus																			
1	2	3	4	5	6	7	8	9	10	11	12	13	14	15	16	17	18	19	20
21	22	23	24	25	26	27													

Numbers																			
1	2	3	4	5	6	7	8	9	10	11	12	13	14	15	16	17	18	19	20
21	22	23	24	25	26	27	28	29	30	31	32	33	34	35	36				

Deuteronomy																			
1	2	3	4	5	6	7	8	9	10	11	12	13	14	15	16	17	18	19	20
21	22	23	24	25	26	27	28	29	30	31	32	33	34						

Joshua																			
1	2	3	4	5	6	7	8	9	10	11	12	13	14	15	16	17	18	19	20
21	22	23	24																

Judges																			
1	2	3	4	5	6	7	8	9	10	11	12	13	14	15	16	17	18	19	20
21																			

Ruth																			
1	2	3	4																

1 Samuel																			
1	2	3	4	5	6	7	8	9	10	11	12	13	14	15	16	17	18	19	20
21	22	23	24	25	26	27	28	29	30	31									

2 Samuel																			
1	2	3	4	5	6	7	8	9	10	11	12	13	14	15	16	17	18	19	20
21	22	23	24																

1 Kings																			
1	2	3	4	5	6	7	8	9	10	11	12	13	14	15	16	17	18	19	20
21	22																		

2 Kings																			
1	2	3	4	5	6	7	8	9	10	11	12	13	14	15	16	17	18	19	20
21	22	23	24	25															

1 Chronicles																			
1	2	3	4	5	6	7	8	9	10	11	12	13	14	15	16	17	18	19	20
21	22	23	24	25	26	27	28	29											

2 Chronicles																			
1	2	3	4	5	6	7	8	9	10	11	12	13	14	15	16	17	18	19	20
21	22	23	24	25	26	27	28	29	30	31	32	33	34	35	36				

Ezra																			
1	2	3	4	5	6	7	8	9	10										

Nehemiah

| 1 | 2 | 3 | 4 | 5 | 6 | 7 | 8 | 9 | 10 | 11 | 12 | 13 |

Esther

| 1 | 2 | 3 | 4 | 5 | 6 | 7 | 8 | 9 | 10 |

Job

1	2	3	4	5	6	7	8	9	10	11	12	13	14	15	16	17	18	19	20
21	22	23	24	25	26	27	28	29	30	31	32	33	34	35	36	37	38	39	40
41	42																		

Psalms

1	2	3	4	5	6	7	8	9	10	11	12	13	14	15	16	17	18	19	20
21	22	23	24	25	26	27	28	29	30	31	32	33	34	35	36	37	38	39	40
41	42	43	44	45	46	47	48	49	50	51	52	53	54	55	56	57	58	59	60
61	62	63	64	65	66	67	68	69	70	71	72	73	74	75	76	77	78	79	80
81	82	83	84	85	86	87	88	89	90	91	92	93	94	95	96	97	98	99	100
101	102	103	104	105	106	107	108	109	110	111	112	113	114	115	116	117	118	119	120
121	122	123	124	125	126	127	128	129	130	131	132	133	134	135	136	137	138	139	140
141	142	143	144	145	146	147	148	149	150										

Proverbs

1	2	3	4	5	6	7	8	9	10	11	12	13	14	15	16	17	18	19	20
21	22	23	24	25	26	27	28	29	30	31									

Ecclesiastes

| 1 | 2 | 3 | 4 | 5 | 6 | 7 | 8 | 9 | 10 | 11 | 12 |

Song of Songs

| 1 | 2 | 3 | 4 | 5 | 6 | 7 | 8 |

Isaiah

1	2	3	4	5	6	7	8	9	10	11	12	13	14	15	16	17	18	19	20
21	22	23	24	25	26	27	28	29	30	31	32	33	34	35	36	37	38	39	40
41	42	43	44	45	46	47	48	49	50	51	52	53	54	55	56	57	58	59	60
61	62	63	64	65	66														

Jeremiah

1	2	3	4	5	6	7	8	9	10	11	12	13	14	15	16	17	18	19	20
21	22	23	24	25	26	27	28	29	30	31	32	33	34	35	36	37	38	39	40
41	42	43	44	45	46	47	48	49	50	51	52								

Lamentations

1	2	3	4	5

Ezekiel

1	2	3	4	5	6	7	8	9	10	11	12	13	14	15	16	17	18	19	20
21	22	23	24	25	26	27	28	29	30	31	32	33	34	35	36	37	38	39	40
41	42	43	44	45	46	47	48												

Daniel

1	2	3	4	5	6	7	8	9	10	11	12

Hosea

1	2	3	4	5	6	7	8	9	10	11	12	13	14

Joel

1	2	3

Amos

1	2	3	4	5	6	7	8	9

Obadiah

1

Jonah														
1	2	3	4											

Micah														
1	2	3	4	5	6									

Nahum														
1	2	3												

Habakkuk														
1	2	3												

Zephaniah														
1	2	3												

Haggai														
1	2													

Zechariah														
1	2	3	4	5	6	7	8	9	10	11	12	13	14	

Malachi														
1	2	3	4											

Pastor Mark Driscoll founded Mars Hill Church (www.marshillchurch.org) in Seattle in the fall of 1996, which has grown to over six thousand people in one of America's least churched cities. He co-founded and is president of the Acts 29 Church Planting Network (www.acts29network.org), which has planted over one hundred churches in the United States and internationally. Most recently he founded the Resurgence Missional Theology Cooperative (www.theresurgence.com).

Outreach magazine has recognized Mars Hill Church as the second most innovative, twenty-third fastest-growing, and second most prolific church-planting church in America. *The Church Report* has recognized Pastor Mark as the eighth most influential pastor in America. His sermons are downloaded a few million times a year. *Seattle* magazine has named Pastor Mark one of the twenty-five most powerful people in Seattle.

Media coverage on Pastor Mark and Mars Hill varies from National Public Radio to *Mother Jones* magazine, the *Associated Press*, the *New York Times*, *Blender* music magazine, *Outreach* magazine, *Christianity Today*, *Preaching Today*, and *Leadership* magazine to ABC Television and the 700 Club.

His writing includes the books *Vintage Jesus, The Radical Reformission: Reaching Out without Selling Out,* and *Confessions of a Reformission Rev.: Hard Lessons from an Emerging Missional Church.* He also contributed to the books *The Supremacy of Christ in a Postmodern World* and *Listening to the Beliefs of Emerging Churches.* Most enjoyably, Mark and his high school sweetheart, Grace, delight in raising their three sons and two daughters.